CU00689393

LEARNING
IN PUBLIC

TRANSEUROPEAN COLLABORATIONS
IN SOCIALLY ENGAGED ART

Learning in Public: transEuropean
collaborations in socially engaged art

Co-published in 2018 by Create
and the Live Art Development Agency
on behalf of the CAPP network.

The CAPP network is led by Create (Ireland),
with Agora Collective (Germany), hablarenarte
(Spain), Heart of Glass (United Kingdom),
Kunsthalle Osnabrück (Germany), Live Art
Development Agency (United Kingdom),
Ludwig Múzeum (Hungary), m-cult (Finland)
and Tate Liverpool (United Kingdom).

Create, 2 Curved Street,
Temple Bar, Dublin, Ireland

Live Art Development Agency (LADA),
The Garrett Centre, Bethnal Green,
London E2 6LX

www.cappnetwork.com

Edited by Eleanor Turney

Designed and illustrated by David Caines

Translations
Spanish to English, Steve Roberts, p. 52-59,
Wade Matthews, p. 84-85
Woloff to Spanish, Ndir El Hadji Sec, P. 85-85
Hungarian to English: Andrea Simon, p. 88-89

Printed and bound by SYL, Barcelona

ISBN: 978-0-9935611-7-7

The drawings of this book have been inspired
by visual documentation of CAPP events that
the nine partner organisations produced
between 2015 and 2018.

Eleanor Turney is a freelance editor, journalist
and arts consultant, and Co-Director of
Incoming Festival. Clients include the
British Council, the BBC, Manchester
International Festival, The Space, Battersea
Arts Centre, Julie's Bicycle, NESTA and the
Donmar Warehouse. She has written for *The
Guardian*, *The Stage*, the *FT*, *The Independent* and
TechCrunch.

David Caines is a graphic designer and visual
artist based in London. Other books he has
designed include *Janine Antoni: Ally* (2017), *Kira
O'Reilly: Untitled (Bodies)* (2017) and *People Show:
Nobody Knows but Everybody Remembers* (2016).
David also makes paintings and in 2015 was
shortlisted for the East London Painting prize.

All rights reserved. The material in this publication is
protected by copyright law. Except as may be permitted by
law, no part of this material may be reproduced (including
by storage in a retrieval system) or transmitted in any
form or by any means: adapted, rented or lent without the
written permission of the copyright owners. Permission
will normally be given to voluntary and community sector
organisations except for commercial purposes.

The European Commission support for the production of
this publication does not constitute an endorsement of the
contents which reflects the views only of the authors, and
the Commission cannot be held responsible for any use
which may be made of the information contained therein.

Contributions © the individual contributors, 2018

Where contributions are dialogues between several
participants, copyright remains with dialogue moderators.

Contents

TIMELINE

December

Partner Meeting #1
Create
Dublin, Ireland

March

Workshop
Werkstattschule
Jorge González
Kunsthalle Osnabrück
Germany

Residency
Art Gym
Assemble and
Tate Collective
Tate Liverpool
Liverpool, UK

Partner Meeting #2
Agora Collective
Berlin, Germany

May

Workshop
Affect #1-5
Stine Marie Jacobsen,
Lorenzo Sandoval,
Yves Mettler,
Diego Agulló, Fotini
Lazaridou-Hatzigoga
Agora Collective
Berlin, Germany
until September, 2015

Workshop
Theatre of Our Bodies
Anna Furse
Create
Dublin, Ireland

2014

2015

Workshop
Kollab Talkshops
Jussi Koitela,
Arttu Merimaa,
Minna Tarkka
m-cult
Helsinki, Finland
until June, 2015

June

Workshop
The Reflective Practitioner
Chrissie Tiller
Tate Liverpool
Liverpool and St
Helens, UK

Partner Meeting #3
m-cult
Helsinki, Finland

July

Workshop
*Everything Under the Sun
series*
Egill Sæbjörnsson,
Dafna Maimon,
Roderick Sloan,
Kultivator, Hanne
Lippard, Natasja
Loutschko, Tue
Greenfort, Thomas
Harttung
Agora Collective
Berlin, Germany
until November, 2015

August

Workshop
DIY 12 series
Zierle & Carter and
Christina Georgiou,
Adam James, Geraldine
Pilgrim, Daniel Oliver,
Shaun Caton, Owen G.
Parry, Ursula Martinez,
Tania El Khoury and
Abigail Conway, Katie
Etheridge and Simon
Persighetti
**Live Art Development
Agency (LADA)**
Locations in UK and
Ireland
until November, 2015

September

Workshop
The Age of Participation
Anita Patonai, András
Sereglei
Ludwig Múzeum
Budapest, Hungary

Workshop
*Laboratory for Urban
Recycling*
Santiago Cirugeda
hablarenarte
Vic, Spain

October

Workshop
Strategies of Non Participation
Karen Mirza
and Brad Butler
Create
Dublin, Ireland

Workshop
If you do not pay attention to me, ...
Sarah Margarita Lewis
hablarenarte
Huarte, Spain

November

Partner Meeting #4
Create
San Servolo, Venice

Workshop
Between Menopause and Old Age
Rocio Boliver
Live Art Development
Agency (LADA)
London, UK

December

Workshop
"I DO" - Gaining by Giving Up
Jakob and
Manila Bartnik
Kunsthalle Osnabrück
Germany
until January, 2016

2015

Workshop
Do it twice
Fermín Jiménez Landa
hablarenarte
San Sebastián, Spain

Residency
With the past in front of me I walk backwards into the future
Louise Lowe
Heart of Glass
St Helens, UK
until May, 2016

Workshop
SEE, THINK, DO
Quad Collective
Tate Liverpool
Liverpool, UK

Public Event
Visible Art Award
Tate Liverpool
Liverpool, UK

January

Workshop
Check Up, Check In
Jesse Jones,
Eleanor Phillips
Create
Dublin, Ireland

Workshop
*The Urban As
Collective Space*
Dos Jotas
hablarenarte
Huarte, Spain

February

Workshop
*Youth Urban
Design Workshop*
Todo Por La Praxis
Create
Callan, Co. Kilkenny,
Ireland

March

Book Launch
Impossible Glossary, ed. 1
various artists
hablarenarte
Madrid, Spain

Workshop
¿All together now?
various artists
hablarenarte
Madrid, Spain

Residency
Baa Baa Baric
Mark Storor
Heart of Glass
St Helens, UK
ongoing

April

Public Event
PLAYING UP
Sibylle Peters
Live Art Development
Agency (LADA)
London, UK

2016

Residency
You are Splendid!
Maria José Arjona
Kunsthalle Osnabrück
Germany
until March, 2016

Workshop
PLAYING UP
Sibylle Peters
Live Art Development
Agency (LADA)
London, UK
until April, 2016

Workshop
*Æctivators. Locally
active architecture*
Levente Polyák,
Dénes Fajcsák
Ludwig Múzeum
Budapest and Eger,
Hungary

Workshop
The Faculty
In Situ & Chrissie Tiller
Heart of Glass
UK

Public Event
You are Splendid!
Maria José Arjona
Kunsthalle Osnabrück
Germany

Exhibition
Art Gym
Assemble and Tate
Collective
Tate Liverpool
Liverpool, UK

Residency
Maunula residencies
Steve Maher, La Jetée,
Riikka Kuoppala,
Thomas Martin,
Valentina Karga, Elena
Mazzi
m-cult
Helsinki, Finland
until November, 2016

Partner Meeting #5
Tate Liverpool
Liverpool, UK

May

Residency
Affect Module I-VI
Judith Lavanga,
Diego Agulló, Lorenzo
Sandoval, Thelma
Bonavita, Sarah
Margarita Lewis
Agora Collective, Berlin
until October, 2016

Residency
Systems of Weight
Ernesto Pujol
Kunsthalle Osnabrück
Germany
until June, 2016

June

Workshop
Prototype Projects:
Artist Social
Emma Fry
Heart of Glass
St Helens, UK

Performance
Systems of Weight
Ernesto Pujol
Kunsthalle Osnabrück
Germany

July

Workshop
Collaborative Arts
with Young Adults
Jennie Guy
hablarenarte
San Sebastian, Spain

Workshop
Hunt and Darton:
Are you Local?
Hunt and Darton
Heart of Glass
St Helens, UK

2016

Residency
Skubi and Bit.Fall
Miklós Tömör, Julius
Popp
Ludwig Múzeum
Budapest, Hungary
until August, 2016

Residency
Candy Star
Juli Reinartz
m-cult
Helsinki, Finland
until June, 2016

Workshop
Dinner Games
YKON group
m-cult
Helsinki, Finland

Workshop
Pleasures and Pains
of Participation
various artists
m-cult
Helsinki, Finland

Residency
Live Art, Privilege
and the Old
Lois Weaver
Live Art Development
Agency (LADA)
London, UK

Exhibition
SKUBI and Bit.Fall
Miklós Tömör, Julius
Popp
Ludwig Múzeum
Budapest, Hungary
until July, 2016

Public Walk
Heavy Metal Detector
Steve Maher
m-cult
Helsinki, Finland

Residency
Live Art, Privilege
and the Young
Sibylle Peters
Live Art Development
Agency (LADA)
London, UK

September

Residency
Resort Residency
Selina Thompson
Create
Fingal, Ireland

Commission
O.K. - The Musical
Christopher Kline
Tate Liverpool
Liverpool, UK
until May, 2017

October

Workshop
Ordinary Landscapes
Francesc Muñoz
hablarenarte
Vic, Spain

Residency
Reflections
Sophie Mahon
Heart of Glass
St Helens, UK
until May, 2017

November

Performance
An Anatomy Act;
A Show and Tell
Anna Furse
Create
Dublin, Ireland

Residency
Research Residency
Anna Furse
Create
Dublin, Ireland
until December, 2016

December

Residency
Live Art, Privilege
and the Displaced
Elena Marchevska
Live Art Development
Agency (LADA)
London, UK

Residency
Live Art, Privilege
and Class
Kelly Green
Live Art Development
Agency (LADA)
London and Kent, UK

Residency
(Re)searching the
Social Element
Michael Birchall,
Warsame Ali Garare
hablarenarte
Madrid, Spain
and November, 2017

Residency
Rethinking the Container
Enter This,
Orekari Collective
hablarenarte
Pamplona, Spain
until June, 2017

Partner Meeting #6
hablarenarte
Valencia, Spain

January

Residency
Harrotu Illeak!
Felipe Polania and
Oihane Espuñez
hablarenarte
San Sebastian, Spain
until July, 2017

Commission
Sounds and Stories Live
Jobina Tinnemans
m-cult
Helsinki, Finland
until February, 2017

February

Commission
I am Hungry:
Related Primates
Dafna Maimon
Agora Collective
Berlin, Germany
until April, 2017

CAPP website launch
Create
Dublin, Ireland

March

Exhibition
Harrotu Illeak!
Felipe Polania and
Oihane Espuñez
hablarenarte
San Sebastian, Spain
until May, 2017

Staging Post #1 and
Partner Meeting #7
Practice, Participation,
Politics
Live Art Development
Agency (LADA)
London, UK

2017

Exhibition
Media works - local
dialogues on global change
Valentina Karga, Elena
Mazzi, La Jetée
m-cult
Helsinki, Finland
until February, 2017

Residency
Meet You at The Green?
Dan Dorocic
Create
Callan, Co. Kilkenny,
Ireland
until April, 2017

Residency
Artist In Residence at
UCD College of Social
Science and Law 2017
Sarah Browne
Create
Dublin, Ireland

Residency
Artist In Residence at
UCD Parity Studios 2017
Glenn Loughran
Create
Dublin, Ireland

Residency
Afluents
Seila Fernández
Arconada, A+
hablarenarte
Vic, Spain
until December, 2017

Performance
Sounds And Stories Live
Jobina Tinnemans
m-cult
Helsinki, Finland

Commission
Artists in Classrooms
various artists
Ludwig Múzeum
Budapest, Hungary
until August, 2017

Commission
Floating House
Bence Zsin
Ludwig Múzeum
Pécs, Rücker-akna lake,
Hungary
until June, 2017

Commission
To be Continued?
Tibor Gyenis
Ludwig Múzeum
Oszkó, Hungary
until October, 2017

April

Commission
Dragon Lee
Tökmag group
Ludwig Múzeum
Komló, Hungary
until October, 2017

Workshop
Dokumentation workshop
Pour Nahid Martin,
Serexhe Berhard,
Müller Dorcas
Ludwig Múzeum
Budapest, Hungary

Performance
Related Primates
Dafna Maimon
Agora Collective
Berlin, Germany

Residency
20:20 Vision
Sophie Mahon
Heart of Glass
until May 2017

Exhibition
Fairground
Kelly Green
Live Art Development
Agency (LADA)
London, UK

May

Exhibition and performance
O.K. - The Musical
Christopher Kline
Tate Liverpool
Liverpool, UK
until May, 2017

Commission
*I am Hungry:
[{"cibelle"(cavalli}bastos)]*
Cibelle Cavalli Bastos
Agora Collective
online
until December, 2017

Commission
I like being a Farmer...
Antje Schiffers,
Katalin Erdődi
Ludwig Múzeum
Nagykamarás,
Körösszegapáti,
Szekszárd, Budapest,
Hungary
until December, 2017

Commission
Reform 75/100
Bernadette Wolbring
m-cult
Helsinki, Finland
until August, 2017

Commission
Arboretum
various artists
Ludwig Múzeum
Budapest, Hungary
until January, 2018

Webinar
CAPP ON AIR #1
Live Art Development
Agency (LADA)

Residency
Research Residency
Sandra Noeth
Create
Dublin and Limerick,
Ireland

Exhibition
20:20 Vision
Sophie Mahon
Heart of Glass
St Helens, UK
until May, 2017

Commission
We Will See!
various artists
Ludwig Múzeum
Budapest, Hungary
until January, 2018

Commission
myfutures.trade
eeefff: group
m-cult
Helsinki, Finland

Commission
Martial Law
Anastasia Artemeva
m-cult
Helsinki, Finland
until September, 2017

May

June

July

August

2017

September

Exhibition
*Mode D: After the Future...
of Work*
Glenn Loughran
Create
Venice, Italy
until October, 2017

Public Event
Baa Baa Baric
Mark Storor
Heart of Glass
St Helens, UK

October

Book Launch
*RRR4, Study Room
Guides and Toolkits*
various artists
Live Art Development
Agency (LADA)
London, UK

Commission
and Public Event
*KAPUTT: The Academy
of Destruction*
Sibylle Peters
Live Art Development
Agency (LADA)
London, UK

November

Exhibition
Afluents
Seila Fernandez
Arconada, Collective A+
hablarenarte
Vic, Spain

Commission
The Forgetting of Air
Francesca Grilli
Kunsthalle Osnabrück
Germany

Staging Post #3 and
Partner Meeting #9
Back to Babel
Kunsthalle Osnabrück
Germany

December

Book Launch
Untitled (Bodies)
Kira O'Reilly
Live Art Development
Agency (LADA)
London, Dublin and
Helsinki

Public Event
PLAYING UP
Sibylle Peters
Kunsthalle Osnabrück
Germany
until October, 2017

Public Event
Martial Law
Anastasia Artemeva
m-cult
Helsinki, Finland

Public Event
Partizaning Maunula
Partizaning group
m-cult
Helsinki, Finland

Talk
I like being a Farmer ...
Antje Schiffers,
Katalin Erdődi
Ludwig Múzeum
Auróra, Hungary

Commission
Untitled (Bodies)
Kira O'Reilly
Live Art Development
Agency (LADA)
London, Dublin and
Helsinki
until December 2017

Public Event
*Against Ordinary
Language*
Sarah Browne,
Leah Marojevic,
Dr. Stuart Murray
Tate Liverpool
Liverpool, UK

January

<u>Staging Post #4</u>
Work in Process
hablarenarte
Madrid, Spain

<u>Exhibition</u>
Common Affairs
various artists
Ludwig Múzeum
Budapest, Hungary
until March, 2018

February

<u>Book Launch</u>
Impossible Glossary ed 2.
various artists
hablarenarte
Madrid, Spain

<u>Exhibition</u>
Sharing processes
various artists
hablarenarte
Madrid, San Sebastian,
Vic, Huarte
until September, 2018

March

<u>Commission</u>
Traveller Collection
Seamus Nolan
Create
Dublin, Ireland
until September, 2018

<u>Commission</u>
I AM Not A Piece Of Meat
Anna Furse
Create

2018

<u>Symposium</u>
*Collaborative
Conversations*
various artists
Tate Liverpool
Liverpool, UK

<u>Residency</u>
*Pathway 2 as part of
The Lives We Live
public art programme*
Brokentalkers
Create
Grangegorman,
Dublin, Ireland
until September, 2018

April

<u>Staging Post #5 and
Partner Meeting #10</u>
*With.For.About: Making
A Meal Of It*
Heart of Glass, Tate
Liverpool
St Helens & Liverpool

<u>Commission</u>
The Mansford Window
Sheaf+Barley
Live Art Development
Agency (LADA)
London, UK
until July, 2018

June

Destination Event
CAPP: Practice and Power
Create with
CAPP partners
Dublin, Ireland

Commission
*Declaration of
Independence*
Barby Asante
Live Art Development
Agency (LADA)
London, UK

May

Webinar
CAPP ON AIR #3
Ludwig Múzeum

September

Commission
Scottee 10
Scottee
Live Art Development
Agency (LADA)
London, UK

Partner Meeting #11
Ludwig Múzeum
Budapest, Hungary

PREFACE

In collaborative processes, beginnings and endings are important. And so it is with the Collaborative Arts Partnership Programme (CAPP). CAPP has its beginnings in 2013, when Create initiated the European Learning Network (ELN) in partnership with Dublin City Council Arts Office, Tate Liverpool (UK), Live Art Development Agency (UK) and m-cult (Finland). The ELN set out to explore the evolving professional development needs of collaborative artists with a view to responding on a European level. In 2014, we were joined by hablarenarte (Spain), Agora Collective (Germany), Kunsthalle Osnabrück (Germany) and Ludwig Múzeum (Hungary), and made a successful bid to the Creative Europe programme of the European Union[1] establishing CAPP as a transEuropean network.

In April 2015, as incoming Director of Create, I joined my first CAPP partner meeting in Berlin. I remember very clearly thinking that this group of people seemed to have been working together much longer than five months. This was in no small part due to the initial planning done to create a robust partnership.

The overall goal of CAPP was to improve and open up opportunities for artists working collaboratively across Europe by enhancing mobility and exchange, whilst engaging new publics and audiences for collaborative practices, thereby increasing awareness and understanding of collaborative arts practice across Europe. CAPP set out to achieve this through professional development workshops in year one, residencies and commissions in years two and three, and raising awareness amongst cultural commentators, venue and gallery managers of the rich potential of collaborative arts through various public dissemination moments in years three and four.

Collaborative processes have a way of finding their own rhythms and ways of working. CAPP was no exception. So, as we considered what kind of publication Learning in Public: transEuropean collaborations in socially engaged art would be, we wanted to relieve it of the burden of representing the totality of the programme. The different phases of the project and the work undertaken by each partner and associate artists are detailed on the CAPP website.[2] Rather, we wanted to reflect the dialogical nature of the work, and to prompt critical questions for the field of collaborative and socially engaged arts, hence our invitation to three leading theorists to contribute to this publication.

In the first essay (p.28), Dr. Mick Wilson adeptly responds to a brief that asked him to consider the field of collaborative and socially engaged practice in Europe, in the context of its current socio-political antagonisms. Wilson proposes a new register for collaborative and socially engaged arts practice which draws on a capacity within the field to manifest a broader political imaginary. He proposes social practice as a mode of constituting *applied experiments in political imagination* and argues powerfully for the relevance of these practices for the times in which we live. He sees their transformative potential not purely in terms of the procedural and the technical, but also at the level of the political imaginary.

Professor Eleonora Belfiore (p.40) tackles the philosophical challenges of measuring and ascribing value in this arena of practice. Belfiore pays close attention to the value of the artist, which is of particular relevance for a network such as CAPP that has had the question of support for collaborative artists at its centre. She asks to what extent that value is assumed or taken for granted, identifying a systemic under-resourcing of the field, which has resulted in a significant invisible subsidy by artists. She points to a moral failure of public policy making, calling for a collective strategy with artists, arts administrators and academics to resist the exploitative tendencies of the art world.

In her essay (p.52), Dr. Aida Sánchez de Serdio Martín poses questions around the notion of archive, and the ongoing challenge of constructing a history or histories of collaborative and socially engaged practice. Sánchez de Serdio opens up the possibility of developing methodologies that call into question traditional history and how it is constructed. By creating an analogy with feminist theory, she proposes instead a community of knowledge made up of meanings and actions that draw us closer but which also allows for our different, even contradictory, narratives. Her argument draws persuasively against the smoothing over of those inevitable fault lines that open up in collaborative practice and points to a history which is based on action research; one which has emerged from collaborative processes where the participation of different actors has been essential.

De Serdio's essay is an apt forerunner to Dr. Susanne Bosch's contribution (p.60). As an artist and CAPP Researcher, Bosch crafted an action research process which was consciously reflexive and discursive. She employed an arts-based methodology for capturing the richness, and indeed the fault lines, which inevitably emerge over a four-year process. Her essay considers CAPP from the point of view of an embedded researcher in the four-year journey of the project.

From the outset, the CAPP partners, artists and communities brought a strong commitment to the principles of negotiation and co-operation, and to the imaginative possibilities that arise when collaboration is employed creatively. Throughout the partner communities, CAPP set out to provide creative spaces with the potential to bring out new conversations, meaningful relationships and transformative forms of collaborative engagement. In this book, we wanted to emphasise the centrality of dialogue to the practice and to our endeavours as a network. The decision-making processes which drove our work were infused by considerations around power, politics, process, participation and place. We take this moment of critical reflection to actively engage with those thematics through five dialogues with artists and project collaborators (pp.83–117).

In Belfiore's essay, artist Sophie Hope speaks of the fluid nature of endings. This may be the case for CAPP as we approach the closing of the project, where the question of legacy is to the fore. Doubtless we can claim a significant body of collaborative initiatives, the residues of our relational matrix and the duty of care as arts organisations that we will need to bring to the afterlife of those projects. But what might be claimed as legacy that goes beyond the immediacy of those shared investments?

The CAPP partners are in active dialogue about a new transEuropean alliance for collaborative and socially engaged arts. The *Practice and Power* conference event in Dublin in June 2018 is the final dissemination moment for CAPP. At this major public gathering we enter into dialogue with the sector – artists, academics, arts organisations and institutions – around what such an alliance might look like. Who is it for and, most importantly, how might it continue to support artists and potential future participants to influence the field of practice? Writer and critic Claire Pentecost has characterised the artist as someone who consents to learn in public.[3] As we embark on the next stage of this journey, post CAPP, we take our lead from that spirit of shared adventure and extend an invitation to others to join and learn with us.

Ailbhe Murphy, Director, Create, May 2018.

1. European Co-operation Project – Creative Europe (Culture Sub Programme) 2014-2018.
2. cappnetwork.com
3. See Pentecost C, *Beyond Face* in Chodos, E., ed. *Talking with Your Mouth Full: New Language for Socially Engaged Art*, Green Lantern, Chicago, 2008, pp.29-45.

WIDER PERSPECTIVES

Applied experiments in political imagination

Mick Wilson

"'Capitalist realism': the widespread sense that not only is capitalism the only viable political and economic system, but also that it is now impossible even to imagine a coherent alternative to it."
(Fisher, Mark, *Capitalist Realism: Is There No Alternative?* Zero Books, 2009, p.2)

"An unfortunate over-philosophication of leftist political debate... has helped create in the universities... a self-involved academic left which has become increasingly irrelevant to substantive political discussion."
(Rorty, Richard, *Response to Ernesto Laclau*, in *Deconstruction and Pragmatism*, ed. Mouffe, Chantal, Routledge, 1996, p.69)

From here to there

This essay seeks to respond to a brief from the CAPP network, and to do so with a certain caution. The brief requires an attempt to outline the state of play with respect to collaborative and socially engaged arts practice in the European context. The brief further suggests that this theme can be treated in relation to practice and an "increasingly acquisitive institutional gaze". In the invitation to contribute to this volume, it is also proposed that there should be a specific engagement with the question of what it might mean to be a socially engaged arts practitioner at a time when, at the level of global geo-politics, we are witnessing vulnerable populations on the move at an unprecedented scale. The invitation underlines that these issues are addressed in a historical moment characterised by a consolidation of familiar exclusionary discourses around forms of ethnicity and identity, particularly at the level of the nation state. Against the backdrop of this historical conjuncture, the questions then posed by the brief are:

"How can artists working collaboratively respond? How can collaborative arts and cultural practices challenge dominant and exclusionary narratives, or indeed, can they do this? How does a transEuropean network such as CAPP create the conditions to extend the field of practice not just geographically but artistically?"

This framing of the invitation to write on social and collaborative art practice describes the current historical moment by moving across a series of different registers: the global geopolitics of migrant flows; the resurgent ethno-national state; the regional cultural-politics of European networks; and collaborative practitioners embedded within societal locations, and operative at the manifold junctures of geography, history, polity, society, economy, culture and biography.

It is worth remarking at the outset that there is a political imaginary at work here that allows the possibility of bridging, in analytical and critical terms (i.e., discursively), but also in practical terms, between vastly different scales. This imaginary posits that the networked micro-practices of collaborative arts production might be usefully apprehended with reference to the grids of geopolitics and the renewed exclusionary propensities of the nation-state, albeit with a sense of the dangers of over-reaching in positioning practices in this way: "can they do this?". Within this scenario, a sense of a growing danger is signalled also by the brief. This danger is nominated in the brief as an "acquisitive institutional gaze" that appears to seek to co-opt, domesticate or otherwise colonise the domain of social and collaborative art practice, when that practice is implicitly conceived as emerging elsewhere, not within the immediate remit of such (acquisitive) institutions.

This way of configuring the question of contemporary socially engaged and collaborative practice has been brilliantly rehearsed by Gregory Sholette, who, over the past two decades, has developed a rigorous and highly considered analysis of the conditions of social practice. Sholette, writing in the North American context but drawing examples from further afield, positions the question of social practice not only with respect to the

genealogies of contemporary art practice, but also with respect to traditions of left political activism and cultural-political dissidence. In his essay *Delirium and Resistance After the Social Turn*",[1] Sholette describes the paradoxical conditions of what, a decade previously, Claire Bishop had nominated as "the social turn":[2]

"That a relationship exists... between the rise of social practice art and the fall of social infrastructures there can be no doubt. And it raises the question, of why art has taken a so-called 'social turn'... just at this particular juncture? ...Engaged art practices appear poised to exit the periphery of the mainstream art world where they have resided for decades, often in the nascent form of 'community arts', in order to be embraced today by a degree of institutional legitimacy... This is not a simple matter of good intentions being co-opted by evil institutions. We are well beyond that point. The co-dependence of periphery and center, along with the widespread reliance on social networks, and the near-global hegemony of capitalist markets makes fantasies of compartmentalizing social practice from the mainstream as dubious as any blanket vilification of the art world."[3]

In order to access the paradoxes of a moment of institutional acquisitiveness with respect to socially engaged practice, Sholette, while looking in detail at particular cases, centralises the theoretical questions of capital and the changing modes of capital ("Capital 2.0")[4] in order to provide the analytical means for his interrogation. Having noted that the road to hell is "undoubtedly paved with many good interventions" he argues that:

"What has changed is the phenomenal aggregation of networked social productivity and cultural labor made available today as an artistic medium, and at a time when society is intellectually, culturally, and constitutively destitute. Art, along with virtually everything else, has been subsumed by capital, resulting in the socialisation of all production... Meanwhile, social practice artists collect the bits and pieces of what was once society like a drawer of mismatched socks. Is it any surprise that these social artefacts only seem to feel alive in a space dedicated to collecting and maintaining historical objects (... the museum)?"[5]

While I am broadly sympathetic to, and aligned with, Sholette's analyses and his wider theoretical framing, I am cautious of the way in which we move quickly and summarily across registers and scales, so as to create – albeit within a dialectic of "paradox" – a unitary systemic co-ordination under the heading of "capital". I am also a little cautious at the way in which a North American world view might so readily become the world view, so that one critique of a globalising hegemony

may risk becoming the globally hegemonic mode of critique. (Of course, I would not want to propose a specifically "European" world-view as an alternative in this regard.)

This is why I am pointing to the theme of the imaginary, and specifically pointing to what I am calling the political imaginary. The critical text (the brief I am given in the invitation to contribute; my response to that brief; Sholette's text) and the various modes and instances of collaborative or socially engaged art practice, proceed upon some form of political imaginary. This political imaginary delimits the sense of what is conceivable, what exists, what is possible, and what is the horizon of hope and despair with respect to power and collectivity for the various agents in play. My gambit, then, is that what makes a certain sub-set of contemporary collaborative and socially-engaged arts practices of especial relevance is that they not only manifest or proceed from a broader political imaginary, but that they also constitute applied experiments in political imagination; they effect operations upon the political imaginary. These applied experiments in political imagination have a transformative potential both in the procedural technical and in the imaginative register.

This is a tentative position that has been developed together with colleagues, through the encounter with the work of many different

artists, theorists and activists. However, it is particularly informed by the work and writing of many different practitioners, including Jeanne van Heeswijk, Kerstin Bergendal, Transparadiso and Kathrin Böhm. It is also informed by a critical rejection of the BAVO critique of NGO art[6] and the all-too-easy rhetorical subsuming of social practice under a generic condemnation of neoliberalism, as the effective externalising of social labour and erosion of social infrastructure. The remainder of this essay seeks, then, to outline a framework for the proposition that certain modes of contemporary collaborative and socially engaged practice constitute *applied experiments in political imagination*. In order to do this, it is necessary to re-visit the core terms in play and consider what work they are doing: What differences are we seeking to signal by invoking "collaborative" and "socially-engaged" practices?

Coming to social terms

There exist a wide range of terms to designate art practices that diverge in different ways from the formal model of the modernist, autonomous work of art. These include 'socially engaged art', 'social practice', 'community art', 'community-based art', 'collaborative practice', 'collaborative art', 'interventionist art', 'dialogic art', 'littoral art', 'relational art', 'contextual art', 'new genre

public art' and 'activist public art'. These terms give prominence variously to the repositioning of spectatorship, collaboration in authorship and/or participation in production. These different emphases on changing the means of production, the modes of exchange and consumption, and the models of encounter with art processes, are most often posited as standing in contrast to the conventional dynamic of the individual's spectatorship (*post facto*) of the artist's completed and self-sufficient authorship. In spite of the sustained critique of the artist-genius model over the past several decades, many see this posited self-sufficiency of the work of art, and the exceptionalism accorded to the radically 'open' vocation of the artist, as still operative within the paradigms of artistic practice inherited in the wake of modernism.

Other themes, foregrounded through the use of the terms listed above, include the incorporation of social, political and economic processes into the artwork as material, production process, outcome and medium. The new nomenclature proposed is an attempt to accommodate the constitution of the work of art by conversation, social encounter, economic transaction, community-building, social relationship, collectivisation, activism, networking, instituting, assembling, local democratic intervention and other forms of self-consciously collective action within the fields of everyday practice. These forms of practice are not restricted to what were previously understood as the 'traditional' and 'appropriate' spaces of art production and distribution, such as the gallery, museum, studio, public park or city square, however they may draw upon these sites.

Furthermore, as has often been pointed out, the widespread growth of social practice overlaps with not only an erosion of other forms of social infrastructure but also an expansion in exhibitionary platforms, scattered-site temporary public art schemes, city marketing through arts festivals, arts based place-making, temporary public art commissioning agencies and changes in arts policy. These overlapping developments seem to provide the conditions of possibility for the greatly expanded field of the social turn in the past two decades.

The terms introduced above are not reducible to each other. Rather, they designate different prioritisation, reflect different historical conjunctions and proceed from different, often countervailing, cultural political projects. For this reason, the terms collaborative and socially engaged arts practices are employed here as a shorthand, not for a monolithic construction, but rather for a distributed and diverse problematic within which, it is claimed, the art institution, art production, art spectatorship and the

distribution of art have been socialised to a greater extent than before. This socialisation has most often been presented as operating in contra-distinction to a perceived hegemonic cultural inheritance. It is typically announced in contrast to the paradigm of fine art as elite social formation, premised on three discrete moments of individuation: the artist, the work, and the viewer. As indicated above, this paradigmatic form may be seen as the hierarchy of agency posited across these three discrete moments: the productive subjectivity of the artist, the emergent self-sufficiency of the work of art (as 'open' in terms of possible experiential, interpretative and discursive appropriations, but also, in some important sense, as self-enclosed), and the receptive/reactive subjectivity of the viewer.

Collaborative and socially engaged arts practices explicitly seek to socialise one or more of these individuated moments, or to in some way displace this tripartite construction by fostering another social grammar of artistic relations. They abandon this construction of discrete moments altogether in favour of entanglements that complicate the art process and weaken the ontology of the work of art.[7]

Given the widespread adoption of these practices, the changed infrastructural conditions of the art system, and the transfer of experience and insight across several generations of practitioners, it is perhaps becoming less necessary for the proponents of the social turn to produce a legitimising counter-narrative to challenge the perceived patrimony of elite art formations. Indeed, as noted above, Sholette and others have underlined the degree to which the social turn entails the institutional legitimisation of collaborative and socially engaged arts practices. However, there persists in some quarters a tendency to produce the social turn as the 'other' of an inherited, and still dominant, 'fine' art system.[8] Janna Graham argues that there is a need to avoid a simplistic construction of 'social art' as a genre in a way that obscures the substantial social functions of the art world as such; the questions of economic and racial injustice that structure its foundation; and the fully social nature of all artistic modes.[9] Graham's declaration that all art is social work is an important rejoinder to the implicit proposition that the traditions of the fine arts might in some way operate outside social reproduction.

This gathering of multiple artistic modes under the broad heading of collaborative and socially engaged practices refers to contradictory tendencies. For example, relational aesthetics and community art may be seen to be diametrically opposed with respect to the valorisation of the artist's role, and with respect to the specification of the relationality that an art practice is supposed to engender or deploy. The various modes of practice itemised above also invoke different genealogies and propose different historicisations of practice. The proponents of 'littoral art practice' may invoke the work of Kurt Schwitters and of the Artists Placement Group; the proponents of 'new genre public art' may invoke feminist performance art and the 'gallery without walls' initiative of earlier champions of cultural democracy; the proponents of 'community art' may invoke *Proletkult;* while other traditions of collaborative practice may propose a rereading of Helio Oiticica, Lygia Clark or Allan Kaprow in the construction of a narrative of emergence for their respective zones and modes of practice.[10]

This means that questions of periodisation and descriptions of tendencies or movements must be treated with caution, as indeed must the whole apparatus of academic art history and art criticism when considering the social turn. Given the strong affinities between the modernist ontology of the discrete work of art, and the conceptual and methodological habits of art historical scholarship and traditional art criticism (which stand in tension with the weakened ontology of the work of art manifest in many of the practices cited above), it is necessary to renew the terms of address with which we position and delimit artistic practice. This is an issue that has long been foregrounded in debates on the social turn, but it nonetheless has not yet been resolved. One virtue with employing a broad designation, such as 'collaborative and socially engaged practices', is that it can serve to foreground the unsettled multiplicity of current practices.

In the next section, however, I depart from this emphasis on multiplicity in order to prioritise one particular dimension of this multiple field, and to underline that subset of practices within this broad setting, which I propose constitute applied experiments in political imagination. In order to do so, it will be necessary to give some greater elaboration of this key term "political imaginary".

From social turn to political imaginary

The terms "social imaginary" and "political imaginary" emerge out of the work of diverse philosophers, cultural historians, and social and political theorists, including Cornelius Castoriadis, Benedict Anderson, Claude Lefort, Drucilla Cornell, Charles Taylor, Wendy Brown and Manfred B. Steger. The slippage between 'social' and 'political' imaginary is in itself an interesting problematic in considering the construction of contemporary social/political imaginaries.

A device often used to exemplify the role of the political imaginary is Benedict Anderson's 1983 reading of national identities in terms of "imagined communities".[11] The political imaginary of nationalism imagines the national community as a collectivity more extensive than any feasible face-to-face community, and therefore requiring imaginative projection through various cultural forms – anthems, flags, rituals, public spectacles, memorials, historical narratives, folk-psychology of 'national character' and other informal belief systems to delimit 'the nation'.

"The nation... is an imagined political community – and imagined as both inherently limited and sovereign. It is imagined because the members of even the smallest nation will never know most of their fellow-members, meet them, or even hear of them, yet in the minds of each lives the image of their communion... In fact, all communities larger than primordial villages of face-to-face contact (and perhaps even these) are imagined. Communities are to be distinguished, not by their falsity/genuineness, but by the style in which they are imagined."[12]

Similarly, projective constructions such as 'the Arabic Spring' or 'Brexit' establish horizons of the thinkable and so produce 'real' effects. In contrast to those theories of ideology that emphasise the distortion of knowledge in ideological processes, the analysis of political imaginaries places greater emphasis on the reciprocally generative role of ideas, values, beliefs, discourses, and political activity, experience and event. Therefore, the political

imaginary is placed outside a true-or-false dichotomy, and does not produce questions of degrees of accuracy or authenticity in representational terms. Political imaginaries are not particularly true or false; they are symbolic forces and processes of meaning-making effecting (not exclusively or determinatively) the conditions of possibility for political action and reciprocally effected by political action in the world. Thus when Mark Fisher describes capitalist realism as "the widespread sense that not only is capitalism the only viable political and economic system, but also that it is now impossible even to imagine a coherent alternative to it",[13] he is addressing the conditions of the contemporary political imaginary.

The capitalist realist reduction of the political to the management of the economy, and the relegation of the social to inconsequential externality, returns to the slippages between social and political imaginaries noted in the genealogy of the term. Arguably, the divisions of the lifeworld into discrete zones or spheres (of the social, the political, the economic, the cultural, the ethical and so forth) is precisely a collaborative imaginative ordering of collective life that undergirds the possibility of a whole range of collective projects from nation-building, profit-seeking and public health to internationalisation, unionisation and sexual dissidence. It is also the case that the re-mapping of this ontology of the lifeworld

is itself a dimension of the contestation of the political imaginary, which has real effect in terms of delimiting what constitutes a meaningful political project and a sense of what is possible.

The significance of the turn to political imaginaries as an analytical strategy lies precisely in the dual nature of this construct: (i) that it does not collapse the pair of 'the imaginary and the real' into the binary of 'the false and the true'; and (ii) that it seems to offer a way to access questions of meaning, symbolism, belief, value and identity as forces effecting the construction of lived worlds, without presuming to stand outside the object of study in the privileged position of ideology critique nor of arrogantly presuming to unmask other people's illusions about themselves and their lifeworld.

Indicative of how this construct has achieved currency in contemporary art are projects such as BAK's *Former West*.[14] This project announces itself as "a long-term, transnational research, education, publishing, and exhibition project in the field of contemporary art and theory". It focuses on "the repercussions of the political, cultural, and economic events of 1989 for the contemporary condition". It uses "the propositional imaginary" of "former West" as a way to challenge the dominant account of political change that speaks of "the former East", and so also challenges the implication that it is the former Soviet sphere that has undergone profound political change, while the hegemonic West remains intact. This is an expanded exhibition project that both discloses and seeks to intervene in the political imaginaries of post-1989 Europe.

However, what specifically interests me here is the possibility that from among the expanding ranks of collaborative and socially engaged arts projects, there are practices that operate as experiments in the collective imagining of alternative ways of living, of co-belonging and of circulating power. Furthermore, I am anxious to differentiate these experiments from the dominant established patterns (there are exceptions) of left intellectual work in the academy, by reference to the applied nature of these practices and their unfolding within the fabric of an institutionally heterogeneous everyday – albeit positioned in complex ways by the intersections of multiple institutional regimes (community, education, health, arts and culture, local economy, local democracy etc.) and by shifting terms of authorship and agency. It is precisely that such complex embedded relationality might be both operated and thematised in a collectively lived practice that is not fully foreclosed, that warrants the claim made by collaborative and social practices on the political imaginary.

This is a highly abstracted claim, and one that risks a certain performative contradiction as an exercise in academic criticism. This claim is proposed not as an argument to students and academic colleagues, but from the experience of collaborating with practitioners in the field, and as a response to these practitioners. It is a proposition to thematise what is being done here, not as a turn to the social, nor as a contestation of modernist autonomous art. Rather, it is as various acts of political imagination that (are not in and of themselves virtuous, but) may, in concert with other actions, and in so much as they are critically problematised, re-constitute the hopes and techniques of collective resistance when much appears hopeless and when the techniques of political organisation seem severely compromised, having been systematically eroded for decades. This is about re-learning the practical techniques of hope that have underpinned the long slow history of struggles for labour, civic, social, economic, legal, racial, sexual and political justice against imagined impossibilities.

Dr. Mick Wilson, artist, educator and researcher, is Head of the Valand Academy of Arts at Gothenburg University, Sweden.

Endnotes

1. Sholette, Gregory, *Delirium and Resistance After the Social Turn*, in *Delirium and Resistance: Activist Art and the Crisis of Capitalism*, ed. Charnley, Kim, Pluto Press, 2017, p.212. The essay originally appeared in *FIELD: an Online Journal of Socially Engaged Art Criticism*, 2015, http://field-journal.com/issue-1/sholette

2. The term 'social turn' was given wide currency by Claire Bishop's 2006 article in *Artforum* and its critical reception in instigating wider debates. This, and an earlier piece by Bishop in the journal *October* from 2004, marked the emergence of a prominent dispute about the first principles and value orientations of modes of practice that sought to displace the modernist ontology of the work of art.

3. Sholette, Gregory, *ibid.*

4. Sholette, Gregory, *ibid.*

5. Sholette, Gregory, *ibid.*

6. BAVO, 2009, *How much politics can art take?*, BAVO Research: www.bavo.biz/texts/view/210

7. "The weakened ontology of the work of art" here refers to the ways in which the discrete boundedness and fixed locus of the work of art becomes dissipated, and the work of art is construed as a dispersed multiple and non-integral framework of experience. This development may be seen to proceed from the widespread adoption of processual, evental, installational and activist modes of artistic production from the 1960s onwards.

8. For a more nuanced and critical reading of these relations, with respect specifically to collectivist forms of practice, see Sholette, Gregory and Stimson, Blake, eds., *Collectivism after Modernism: The Art of Social Imagination after 1945*, Minneapolis, MN: University of Minnesota Press, 2007.

9. See her essay *In the Place of a Placement: Reading Art as Already Social Work in the Practices of the Artist Placement Group* in the forthcoming volume *Public Enquiries: PARK LEK and the Scandinavian Social Turn*, Black Dog Press, 2018.

10. There is a wide-ranging body of literature available that explores and employs these different terminologies, providing different constructions to the genealogy of practices that are here broadly gathered under the heading of 'the social turn'. A partial listing includes: Barber, Bruce, *Sentences on Littoral Art*, Bruce Barber, 1998, http://www.brucebarber.ca/novelsquat/sentences.htm, accessed 4 March 2017; Birchall, Michael G, *Socially engaged art in the 1990s and beyond* in *On Curating*, no.25, May 2015; Bishop, Claire, ed., *Participation*, London: Whitechapel Gallery, 2006; Bourriaud, Nicolas, *Relational Aesthetics*, Dijon: Les presses du réel, 2002; Doherty, Claire, ed., *Contemporary Art from Studio to Situation*, London: Black Dog Publishing, 2004; Doherty, Claire, ed., *Out of Time. Out of Place: Public Art (Now)*, London: Art Book, 2015; Finkelpearl, Tom, *What We Made: Conversations on Art and Social Cooperation*, Durham, NC: Duke University Press, 2013; Jackson, Shannon, *Social Works: Performing Art, Supporting Publics*, New York, NY: Routledge, 2011; Jacob, Mary Jane, Brenson, Michael and Olson, Eva M, *Culture in Action: A Public Art Program of Sculpture Chicago*, Seattle, WA: Bay Press, 1995; Kester, Grant, *Conversation Pieces: Community and Communication in Modern Art*, Berkeley, CA: University of California Press, 2004; Kester, Grant, *The One and the Many: Contemporary Collaborative Art in a Global Context*, Durham, NC: Duke University Press, 2011; Kwon, Miwon, *One Place after Another: Site-Specific Art and Locational Identity*, Cambridge, MA: The MIT Press, 2002; Lacy, Suzanne, *Mapping the Terrain: New Genre Public Art*, Seattle, BA: Bay Press, 1995; Lacy, Suzanne, *Time in Place: New Genre Public Art a Decade Later* in *The Practice of Public Art*, Cartière, Cameron and Willis, Shelly eds., New York, NY: Routledge, 2008; Purves, Ted, ed., *What We Want Is Free: Generosity and Exchange in Recent Art*, Albany, NY: State University of New York Press, 2005; Roberts, John, *Collaboration as a Problem of Art's Cultural Form*, *Third Text*, vol. 18, no. 6, 2004, pp.557–564.

11. Anderson, Benedict, *Imagined communities: reflections on the origin and spread of nationalism*, Verso Books, 1983.

12. *ibid.* p.7.

13. Fisher, Mark, *Capitalist Realism: Is There No Alternative?*, Zero Books, 2009, p.2.

14. www.formerwest.org

The hidden costs of the "re-enchantment of art"
Eleonora Belfiore

Writing in 1991, and building on her previous critique of modernism's aesthetics, artist and critic Suzi Gablik offered a prediction for the future development of art which has proved remarkably acute:

"If modern aesthetics was inherently isolationist, aimed at disengagement and purity, my sense is that what we will be seeing over the next few decades is art that is essentially social and purposeful, art that rejects the myths of neutrality and autonomy. The subtext of social responsibility is missing in our aesthetic models, and the challenge of the future will be to transcend the disconnectedness and separation of the aesthetic from the social that existed within modernism".[1]

The intervening quarter of a century has indeed witnessed a remarkable growth in prominence of what is commonly referred to as socially engaged arts practice – participatory in nature, and with a clear intention to act as intervention in the social and political sphere. In Sophie Hope's definition, as "artist-led, non-object-based encounters, performances, and collaborations with others".[2] Most notably, compared to the radical and fringe status this form of artistic practice had when it developed as part of the 1960s and 1970s countercultural movement, socially engaged arts practice,

and more generally initiatives that are aimed at fostering arts engagement through collaboration and participation, have been increasingly featuring among the range of activities that receive public financial support. Historically, this support has been justified by a renewed focus, on the part of policy makers, on the societal benefits of active participation in arts and culture, and the promise that they might support wider strategies to foster social cohesion and inclusion.

The tactic of using 'social impact' as a proxy for 'value' in making the case for arts funding has proved to be, at best, a double-edged sword;[3] yet it is beyond question that seeing the delivery of social benefits as a sufficiently compelling rationale to warrant and justify public subsidy has resulted in socially engaged arts practice now being more visible (if never adequately supported) within contemporary arts provision. Elsewhere, I have referred to this historical development as "defensive instrumentalism": a self-justifying strategy to be deployed at a time in which traditional rationales for arts funding are seen as no longer holding water with either public or politicians.[4] On the face of it, the current quest for arts with social benefits might appear as the realisation of Gablik's vision[5] for "the emergence of a more participatory, socially interactive framework for art", and "the transition from the art-for-art's-sake assumptions of late modernism, which kept art as a specialised pursuit devoid of practical aims and goals".

Yet, I would argue, reality is more complicated than it appears at first glance. Whilst the move of participatory and socially engaged practice from its 1970s niche of 'community arts' to the mainstream of national and local arts provision is a phenomenon to be celebrated in many respects, it has not come to pass without issues and problems.

In this essay, I intend to explore some such issues and problems. Not because I do not see the value of socially engaged arts practice – quite the opposite. Many of the observations that will follow have been developed through my experiences researching the practice of – and, more recently, working with – socially engaged practitioners. Over the past couple of years, I have had the immense privilege of collaborating (alongside fellow academics and colleagues from the artist development organisation Counterpoints Arts) with several socially engaged artists from a migrant or refugee background as part of the *Who Are We?* exhibition that took place at Tate Exchange, Tate Modern in March 2017, a collaborative endeavour as part of the Tate Exchange Programme.[6] These are all artists whose

practice has involved collaborations with refugees in Calais and other camps, displaced communities, people fleeing war and torture, and generally those facing unimaginable challenges. The resulting artworks, often the product of an active collaboration between artists and communities, have been some of the most moving and affecting I have ever experienced, and audience evaluations seem to suggest my experience was not unique in this respect.[7] What follows is indeed a tribute to the commitment, dedication and the labour of love that these and many other socially engaged artists feed into their practice, and a token of my appreciation for their generosity with their time, experiences and candid conversations.

The strategy that I have referred to as 'defensive instrumentalism' and its concern for the delivery of socio-economic benefits through the arts as a legitimating tactic, has resulted in a focus on the participants in the collaborative endeavour that is socially engaged arts practice. Consequently, much of the debate, both within the sector and in academia, has long focused on the degree to which social impacts resulting from participation might be evaluated, measured and quantified, in line with funders' and politicians' expectations and demands. Time, resource and energy have all gone into the critique of current evaluating frameworks and tools, the quest for better ones, and the assessment of the improvements made in our grasp of how the arts impact participants – or indeed, lack thereof.[8]

I would like to offer a different, yet complementary, discussion to those prevalent in arts and cultural policy circles, by focusing attention on the other partner in this collaborative endeavour: artists. As a policy scholar, I am inevitably fascinated by the policy-making and administrative implications that such a shift in perspectives brings with it, and the moral, political and social justice issues it poses. It is my contention that a better awareness of these is key to the mission of developing more effective ways of working within collaborative and participatory arts practice, and enhancing the opportunities for artists working collaboratively in Europe and beyond.

Placing the spotlight on artists

What follows here is a personal reflection borne out of my experience researching aspects of socially engaged arts practice over the past 15 years, and particularly through an emerging collaboration with photographer and socially engaged artist Eva Sajovic.[9] As part of the collaborative endeavour resulting in the already mentioned *Who Are We?* project

in 2017, we worked together on a Learning Lab entitled *Unlearning the role of the artist*, in which Sajovic reflected on the art of 'unlearning' common preconceptions about the role, function and power of the artist, whilst also posing challenging questions about "the politics of representing others in an age of global displacement".[10] The Learning Lab took the form of a performed auto-ethnography by the artist followed by contributions from critical respondents, rapporteurs (including myself), and open debate with the Lab participants. One of the key questions the event explored was:

What support can artists expect from commissioning organisations when using participatory methodologies, knowing that the boundary between the artist-as-professional and artist-as-friend in process-based participatory work is fluid, blurred and prone to misinterpretation?[11]

This is a question that I had already been grappling with for some time, from the perspective of a cultural policy researcher. I agreed with Sajovic about the highly problematic nature of its neglect in current policy and sector debates – at least public ones, for it had become clear by then that this is in fact a question that practitioners have long been discussing amongst themselves. An emerging collaboration started precisely from this shared unease about the dearth

of public discourse around the contexts and the conditions in which socially engaged practice involving vulnerable individuals and communities takes place. This essay is an opportunity to begin to articulate a series of key points which make up both a research agenda for the future and a space for political campaigning for better working conditions for artists working in a participatory practice.

Like many other cultural labourers, artists share the precariousness, and the exploitative and self-exploitative nature, of creative work. The working conditions of cultural and creative workers have been well documented, alongside the ways in which socioeconomic background still remains a factor in accessing creative careers.[12] We also know that the precariousness, informality and demand for flexibility that characterise this type of work have particularly negative impacts on women, disabled people and minorities.[13] We similarly know that, notwithstanding its fundamental shift from the counter-cultural fringe to the publicly subsidised mainstream, socially engaged arts practice remains structurally under-funded, especially in our present times of post-financial crash austerity.

The question of resourcing participatory and socially engaged practice in a way that could provide the community arts movement with a chance of sustainability has been a long-standing issue: in 1978, Su Braden, in her seminal book *Artists and People*, had already identified the growth of public funding as a very mixed blessing, and as a form of intervention that was altering the radical nature of the activities being carried out, whilst doing nothing to ensure the long term sustainability of the work of artists in communities. Braden lamented the funders' failure to accept that a genuine commitment to the agenda of community arts entailed "a long-term commitment from them as administrators and that this commitment necessitates patient year-by-year programming in which communities and artists can grow together".[14]

This vision of an organic approach to nurturing collaborative arts practice was destined to remain unfulfilled: in 1984, Owen Kelly was already writing about community arts' "grant addiction", the resulting dependency on funders, and the inevitable embrace of their priorities and agendas on the part of the recipients of funding. More recently, Sophie Hope has discussed the persisting problems posed by the prevailing short-term, project-based approach to the socially engaged arts commission.[15] She suggests, moreover, that professionalisation and the reliance on one-off funding grants might be at least in part responsible for the less politically radical inclination of much contemporary socially engaged arts practice, for "there are funders to please and careers to protect and so rocking the boat too much might jeopardise future funding and commissions".[16] She also argues that project-based funding does not sit comfortably with socially engaged artists' preference for fluid structure and naturally evolving collaborative activities. This means that pinpointing exactly when a project 'ends' is not always straightforward (as the running out of the funding does not always coincide with the natural conclusion of the activity), so that attending to the aftercare process for both artists and community participants is not always possible within the scope of the project, as understood in terms of the timescales and expectations of a grant.

Something that emerged powerfully for me a few years ago, when conducting a piece of research on a participatory heritage project involving the Gypsy and Traveller community in Lincolnshire, was the extent to which all of the artists involved, as well as the project managers and communications specialist, reported – unprompted – having contributed to the project a disproportionate amount of free labour, in order to be able to deliver a successful programme of activities and so as to fulfil the expectations they felt the project had created in the participants. The driver was, clearly, commitment to the communities who had placed their trust in them, by allowing their children to be involved in a project exploring and communicating their cultural values, and in spite of previous traumatic experiences of having their culture exposed for the amusement of the entire nation through TV programmes such as *My Big Fat Gypsy Wedding*.[17]

One of the community artists employed on the project talked very candidly and emotively about her difficulties in letting go of the relationships formed through the project, to the extent that, almost two years after the conclusion of the project, she was still offering guidance, creative mentoring and psychological support to one of the young project participants. She was honest about the implications, both material and psychological, that this had for her; as a low-income single mum working freelance, the emotional labour invested in the extra care for her participant was time that could have otherwise be billed for. However, it was clear that the real toll was the weight of responsibility she felt for the welfare of a young girl facing the well-known challenges that young people from a Gypsy and Traveller background routinely face. Never having received training to deal with situations which normally are the domain of professional social workers, she reported being plagued by self-doubt and anxiety: was she offering the right kind of support? Was a well meaning intervention what this kid really needed? Could it be counterproductive? How long could she go on offering this support, when she herself had more of her fair share of responsibilities for her own dependants?

The heartfelt dedication towards the notion of duty of care for participants emerged from all the interviews I conducted as part of this small scale project, and it unleashed a series of questions that I have tried to explore ever since: whose burden should participants' after care *really* be? If, as it seems to be the case, it is effectively artists who often end up taking charge of such duties, should they not be trained to do this safely and appropriately? And most crucially, should not this emotional labour be acknowledged, recognised and suitably remunerated? Unsurprisingly, this invisible labour was something that the artists in the *Who Are We?* collective were very familiar with, too, and which they had taken on in extremely challenging geo-political contexts.

This invisible emotional labour seems such a recurring feature of the working conditions of artists who practice collaboratively with communities (and often with communities facing social disadvantage, discrimination, displacement and other complex challenges), that it is worth reflecting on in more depth. The cultural labour literature highlights the inequalities entailed in a creative career path predicated on beginnings made up of unpaid internships, and labour exchanged for contacts, networking opportunities and visibility rather than payment. However, what we see in the subsidised socially engaged arts practice is a *systemic* under-resourcing that affects practitioners well beyond their early careers. This, alongside the problems we have seen resulting from funding-by-project, effectively means that socially engaged arts practice can survive only because of what we may call an 'invisible subsidy' on the part of the artists themselves at all stages of their careers.

Whilst artists' invisible subsidy might not have been commonly labelled as such, the phenomenon itself is nothing new. However, at least in the UK, the tacit expectation on the part of funders that artists will shoulder the extra burden of project after-care is further compounded by the consequences of a prolonged austerity policy. As noted by the Warwick Commission report, the contraction of welfare provision has significantly reduced the welfare support that had traditionally benefitted both artists and the communities with which they work in socially engaged practice.[18]

These working conditions and the matter of invisible subsidy pose a problem which is two-fold. On the one hand, we have the practical problem of sustainability of artists' careers and their own psychological wellbeing, and on the other, their implication for the moral and political economy of arts subsidy.

What should policy do?

"To create today is to create with responsibility."

This was Suzi Gablik's motto for the renewed, participatory aesthetics she called for in *The reenchantment of art*.[19] She wrote this with artists in mind, but I would argue that we need to extend this expectation to the agencies that are part of the bureaucratic infrastructure of arts support and provision, if we are to ever realise Gablik's vision for "a new connective, participatory aesthetic" and "a value-based art". The weight of responsibility that Gablik refers to needs to be shared out more equally

than it is at present; it is currently artists working in socially engaged contexts, as we have seen, who shoulder the costs of rigorous and respectful practice which fall between the cracks of project funding.

We need an explicit effort to bring our public cultural institutions to task in relation to what Mark Banks calls "creative justice",[20] by highlighting the mechanisms of systemic exploitation of artists within a funding infrastructure that is very comfortable using the rhetoric of collaborative, participatory and socially engaged arts practice, but does not quite follow those principles in its own conduct. Current funding practices, and the ways in which project-based funding rarely incorporates, as a matter of course, provisions to ensure the fulfilment of duties of care towards both artists and participating communities, are a key example of these ethically questionable practices.

In this context, it is crucial that we develop fresh thinking on *the moral economy of the subsidised arts sector*. As Mark Banks observes, "[w]ork is always subject to the norm and values of the particular society in which it is *embedded*", (emphasis in the original).[21] Moral economy approaches help "emphasising the *normative environments* that both ground and

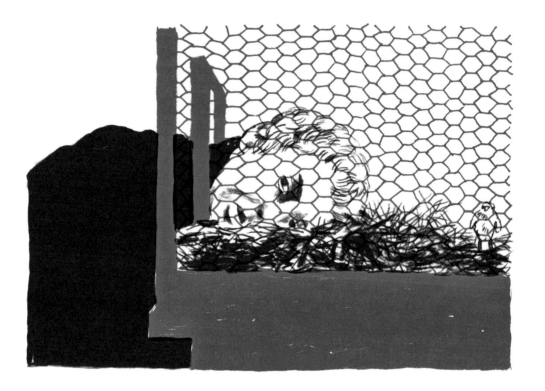

connect different individuals, institutions and structures".[22] It is my contention that the normative environments of contemporary arts funding point to a clear moral failure of cultural policy. Here are the grounds for such a conclusion:

• Poorly funded socially engaged arts practice is too often relied upon to provide evidence, case studies, support and legitimacy for arguments around the social benefits of the arts that are deployed by the (much better funded) arts establishment to help 'make the case for the arts', thus offering fodder for advocacy based on what I have referred to as 'defensive instrumentalism'.

• This, in turn, effectively reinforces patterns of funding that advantage established public arts institutions whilst keeping socially engaged forms of activity under-resourced. Practitioners find themselves thus open to exploitation and self-exploitation, driven by a sense of responsibility towards project participants and their wellbeing during the project – and often well beyond its conclusion (or at least beyond the expiration of the funding).

• In other words, the prevalent strategy for the legitimation of discursive formations that aspire to justify arts subsidy is predicated on the systematic exploitation of cultural workers involved in publicly funded socially engaged practice. In reality, the most precarious, lowest paid cultural workers heavily subsidise the public cultural sector via their poorly paid or unpaid work, their invisible and unacknowledged emotional labour, and by bearing the hidden but significant psychological costs of duty of care towards project participants.

Cumulatively, I would argue, these issues amount to a moral failure of public policymaking, and a betrayal of the official rhetoric the arts sector deploys, with its foregrounding of the values of collaboration, inclusion, transparency and fairness. This is the challenge we need to address if we want to see socially minded collaborative and participatory arts work flourish.

What, then, might the way forward be, if we are genuinely committed to the goal of an aesthetic practice driven by responsibility and a truly collaborative ethos? We need a willingness to hold public institutions and funders to account in the name of fairness and social justice, even when this might lead to uncomfortable conversations with funders, policy-makers and cultural sector partners. This can only ever work as a collaborative strategy, however. Resisting the exploitative tendencies of the arts funding infrastructure cannot be a task reserved for arts practitioners alone. Success will only be achievable through a collective strategy, and the coming together of different actors: artists, for sure, but also academics, arts administrators committed to progressive change within the sector, and – crucially – international coalitions of values and interests much like the one this book documents.

Dr. Eleonora Belfiore is Professor of Communication and Media Studies at Loughborough University.

Endnotes

1. Gablik, Suzi, *The reenchantment of art*, Thames and Hudson, New York, 1991, pp.4-5

2. Hope, Sophie, *From community arts to the socially engaged art commission*, in A. Jeffers and Moriarty, G. (eds.) *Culture, Democracy and the Right to Make Art: The British Community Arts Movement*, 2017, pp.203-221

3. Belfiore, Eleonora, *"Defensive instrumentalism" and the legacy of New Labour's cultural policies* in *Cultural trends*, 21(2), 2012, pp.103-111

4. Belfiore, Eleonora, *ibid.*

5. Gablik, Suzi, *The reenchantment of art*, Thames and Hudson, New York, 1991, pp.4-5

6. *Who Are We?* was produced by Loughborough University, the Open University and the University of Warwick www.whoareweproject.com

7. Tiller, C, *Who Are We? Tate Exchange – First Year Evaluation*, unpublished, 2017

8. Crossick, G. & Kaszynska, P, *Understanding the value of arts & culture: The AHRC Cultural Value Project*, Arts and Humanities Research Council, 2016

9. www.evasajovic.co.uk

10. www.whoareweproject.com/seminars-workshops/2017/3/14/learning-lab-eva-sajovics-unlearning-the-role-of-the-artist

11. *Ibid.*

12. Banks, Mark, *The politics of cultural work*, Springer, 2007

13. Conor, B, Gill, R & Taylor, S, *Gender and creative labour* in *The Sociological Review*, 63 (1_suppl), 2015, pp.1-22

14. Braden, Su, *Artists and People*, Routledge, 1978, p.124

15. Hope, Sophie, *From community arts to the socially engaged art commission* in A. Jeffers and Moriarty, G. (eds.) *Culture, Democracy and the Right to Make Art: The British Community Arts Movement*, Bloomsbury, 2017, pp.203-221,

16. Hope, Sophie, *ibid.*

17. For a fuller discussion of this project, please see Belfiore (forthcoming).

18. Neelands, J, Belfiore, E, Firth, C, Hart, N, Perrin, L, Brock, S, Holdaway, D and Woddis, J, *Enriching Britain: Culture, Creativity and Growth*, the 2015 report by the Warwick Commission on the Future of Cultural Value, The University of Warwick, 2015

19. Gablik, Suzi, *The reenchantment of art*, Thames and Hudson, New York, 1991

20. Banks, Mark, *Creative justice: Cultural industries, work and inequality*, Pickering & Chatto, 2017

21. Banks, Mark, *ibid.*

22. Banks, Mark, *ibid.*

Alone in paradise? History as a way of building a debate and learning community in collaborative art practices

Aida Sánchez de Serdio Martín

This text is the result of a personal, situated realisation. After more than ten years of courses, encounters, projects and dialogues in collaborative art practices, I've begun to feel that I belong to another generation. Perhaps it is this that makes me feel certain debates are needed, for example around history and precursors. In this text, I will discuss some of the factors which may be behind the relative scarcity of historical narratives in the field, and what building such narratives would involve, using feminist theory as a resource.

Where are the histories of collaborative art practices?

One factor we can point to in the production of collaborative art theory is that conceptual debate is much more abundant than historical. We can understand this through the relative youth of collaborative art. This gives it a greater urgency in developing terminology and concepts with which to work out and theorise its practices – and also to legitimise itself and make itself intelligible in the art history context – than in building a historiographical debate about its genealogies.[1]

This absence of historical narratives contrasts with the artistic field in general, which has a long historicising tradition and a discipline – art history – now dating back several centuries. However, it isn't my intention here to claim a place for collaborative art practices within the dominant narratives of art history, based on great figures, the succession of art movements, etc. This is a way of making history that has been widely called into question from within the field itself. My point here is rather (as Griselda Pollock remarked about feminist interventions in art history) that embracing these practices should also involve a paradigm shift:

"Is adding women to art history the same as producing feminist art history? Demanding that women be considered not only changes what is studied and what becomes relevant to investigate, but it changes the existing discipline politically. Women have not been omitted through forgetfulness or mere prejudice. The structural sexism of most academic disciplines contributes actively to the production and perpetuation of a gender hierarchy."[2]

The fact that we speak and write about collaborative art practices as if they lacked models and precedents may be due to the very real absence of documentation endemic in the field (and where it does exist there is a serious lack of orderly compilation). Collaborative art processes tend to be ephemeral, non-material and relational, and are therefore difficult to record even when the will to do so exists, and tend not to produce works easily stocked in museums or reproduced in publications.[3] Also, collaborative art practices, new arrivals on the art scene (with some differences, depending on the context), face difficulties fitting in with the art system's prevailing modes of production, distribution and reception, and are always suspected of being aesthetically and politically unsound: too communitary, too reparative to be really radical and critical.[4]

But aside from these factors which come with the territory, the negation/renunciation of models also echoes artists' uneasy relationship with their forebears and influences, particularly since the beginning of the modernist era. Furthermore, these are sometimes camouflaged by the argument of the incommensurability of contexts and modes of intervention. Perhaps the writer who has best theorised this unease is Harold Bloom in *The Anxiety of Influence*.[5] Bloom argues that writers are anxious that they will not be able to break free from their precursors' influence and therefore have to engage in an Oedipal struggle with them to assert the value of their own writing.

Feminist criticism quickly picked up on the patriarchal, Freudian paradigm underpinning Bloom's analysis and called it into question. In *The Madwoman in the Attic*[6] Sandra Gilbert and Susan Gubar argue, against Bloom, that nineteenth-century women writers experienced rather a *lack* of role-models, since their male precursors embodied a patriarchal model which left them no space as writers or creators. Thus their anxiety stems not from the need to break free of their forebears' influence, but rather from the challenge of exercising authority – i.e. creative authority – in a traditionally masculine field such as literature. Gilbert and Gubar ask what conditions enable women writers to trace and lay claim to a strong matrilineal literary heritage, recovering their forgotten foremothers:

"We will have to trace the difficult paths by which nineteenth-century women overcame their "anxiety of authorship," repudiated debilitating patriarchal prescriptions, and recovered or remembered the lost foremothers who could help them find their distinctive female power."[7]

These debates can also be applied to other art fields, not only because they help us understand the unease artists feel about recognising influences, precedents and lineages in practice, but also because, as Gilbert and Gubar contend, there is no reason why artists' relationships with their precursors should be embodied in struggle when they may also be a source of agency. This is especially true when working in a field where there seem to be few models and the prevailing ones call collaborative art practices themselves into question.

Possible archives, possible histories

The price of not having a history is that we are forced to move forward in solitude and uncertainty, and run the risk of constantly reinventing the wheel. At the same time, our community of debate is impoverished and we're deprived of help from our present and past comrades in analysis and collective action. The question is: what ways of making history do we want for collaborative art practices once we've rejected patriarchal narratives and their geniuses, heroes and father figures? Donna Haraway argues that there is no necessary ethical or political security in subaltern positions, since these are subject to the same complexities and contradictions as the dominant identities they challenge.[8] A history of collaborative

art practices, which we could argue are still peripheral to the art world,[9] cannot trust that its minority position is a guarantee against reproducing new dominant narratives and orthodoxies when assembling a possible history. How can we narrate our own emergence from a standpoint of fragility and uncertainty, and at the same time equip ourselves (to paraphrase Gilbert and Gubart) with a subaltern heritage of creative strength and political agency? Feminist theory, once again, can help us imagine the possibilities.

By "fragility and uncertainty", I'm not only referring to a subjective-political position but also a material-epistemological condition. The existence of a possible history or histories of collaborative art practices depends on the sources, documents, stories and subjects which can enable us to build such a history/histories. But our experiences of the recovery (or even simple subsistence) of sources registering subaltern lifestyles, creativity and political agency reveal the precariousness and instability of the "data" we need for constructing their history.

For example Laura Cottingham, in the introduction to *Not for Sale*, her video-essay on the feminist art experiments of the 70s,[10] defines the piece as "the story of a revolution found in video tapes, memories, slide

collections and telephone conversations," revealing the dispersion and material evanescence of the documents which she had to use to build her narrative. And in an explanatory text, after arguing for the need to situate feminism, along with other resistance and civil rights movements, within the historical process in order to transform the present, she adds:

"As with any historical project, documentation – the literal materiality of the documents, including their accessibility, readability, and reproduction quality – greatly influenced [...] the parameters of my own knowledge as a researcher [...]. Because so few women had commercial support for their art during the 1970s, a sizeable amount of the artworks I located had been reproduced and preserved according to substandard technical conditions."[11]

Thus, the sociopolitical status of the historical processes studied conditions the material circumstances of their documentation and thereby our chances of producing knowledge about them. Subaltern historical phenomena (precisely because they are subaltern) can't guarantee good conservation of the documentation they produce, and therefore this affects the possibilities of archiving them and drawing on them later. This means that

the construction, conservation, organisation and interpretation of archives on collaborative art should be an essential line of analysis, along with that of historicisation, allowing similar debates, such as those on subaltern archives, to orient us.[12]

When there is a lack of documentation and the phenomena studied are still recent, the oral testimony of those involved is essential for historical reconstruction. This is a practice which feminism has both resorted to and criticised. While it's a means of gaining access to non-documented or ignored topics and presenting diversified views of the past, its stress on the value of experience runs a twofold risk. The first is of seeing testimony as affording us a more authentic version of history. The second is of reproducing the hierarchical division of labour between those who experience something, and those who have the power to interpret it and give it meaning.[13]

To these concrete problems, we should add a more general reflection on the implications of challenging the methodological certainties of traditional history in this way. These include problems in defining the categories to be used; the locating, reliability and interpretation of sources; the explanation of the motivation of the processes; and the possibility of synthesising in a constantly more diversified field.[14]

Building a history of collaborative art practices presents similar challenges. Our experiences are mostly immaterial and dispersed; not all are documented, much less historicised. A few publications have included historical cases in compilations of practices (for example *Magic Moments*, on collaboration between artists and young people)[15] and artist monographs (such as *Art for Change*, on the career of Loraine Leeson).[16] There have also been occasional exercises in archiving and archaeology, such as *Transductores*, a project embracing both archiving and intervention, and research projects, which began in Granada (Spain) but now includes cases from a range of different areas.[17] There is also the Cultural Archaeology project, a collective research process initiated by the art and research platform Vagabond Reviews with the Fatima Mansions community in Dublin (Ireland) with the goal of documenting and interpreting the collective process of artistic creation and urban transformation this neighbourhood experienced from the mid-1990s to 2008.[18] Thus initiatives such as CAPP, which not only foster the realisation of collaborative projects but also devise different ways of documenting them, are a vital contribution to the construction of this archive of cases which confirms that – luckily – we are not alone in paradise.

However, as well as having access to specific studies and archives, it's necessary to undertake systematic and situated historical interpretation of these and many other experiences. The goal when constructing this history or histories is not to provide an orthodox narrative which finally establishes a genealogy of influences, nor to raise the field to the level of other art practices in order to gain legitimacy. Rather it's a question of confronting the challenges together that I mentioned previously, in relation to methodologies which set out to call traditional history into question. In doing this, we would be constructing a community not based on dogma or on a consensus around what is already given, but on debate about what is yet to come. By recovering and investigating past and present practices, by comparing and contrasting our ideas and experiences, by putting forward different solutions to each problem, we contribute to making the web of meanings and actions which draws us together denser, even in disagreement. This is, in the end, what constitutes a community of knowledge.

Therefore I imagine a plural and complex history which would analyse the interweaving of the specific narratives of each geopolitical context in the framework of the global circulation of discourses, resources and agents. It would be a living history in the sense that it would be built from present experience, but also because it would necessarily be based on fragile recordings of short-lived actions, and on the testimony of people and groups both past and present. This history, instead of aspiring to enshrine a succession of peak moments or heroic endeavours, would populate our past and present with travelling companions who would help us situate ourselves in a shared territory of either affinity or opposition – or all the shades in between. It would not be an expert-made history, or at least not wholly, but rather based on action-research and collaborative research processes, in which the participation of different actors is essential. It would be articulated around particular cases and turning points rather than continuity and causality, and would be in constant process of reformulation.

A history of which, for now, we still have to talk about in future and conditional terms, but contributed to by every project producing shareable documentation, by every researcher rummaging round in boxes of disorganised documents in order to produce a story. Messages in bottles that one day we will gather together to bind to the fragmentary and multiple threads of a minor history, in order to give meaning to the diverse communities of practice we build with our daily work.

Dr. Aida Sánchez de Serdio Martín is Assistant Professor at the Open University of Catalonia (Universitat Oberta de Catalunya). This essay was translated by Steve Roberts.

Endnotes

1. Although we should mention a number of models such as Suzanne Lacy's *Mapping the Terrain*, Grant Kester's *Conversation Pieces*, Tom Finkelpearl's *What We Made* and Claire Bishop's *Artificial Hells*, all of which devote at least one chapter to historical reconstruction.

2. Pollock, Griselda, *Vision and Difference. Femininity, Feminism and the Histories of Art*, Routledge, London and New York, 1988, p.1.

3. On the other hand, a genre such as performance art, which has similarly process-oriented and ephemeral features, and is also difficult to represent in a museum, has produced historical studies and even comprehensive retrospectives. See the bibliographical entry on the field in Oxford Bibliographies: http://www.oxfordbibliographies.com/view/document/obo-9780199920105/obo-9780199920105-0047.xml and the MoMA exhibition *100 Years. A History of Performance Art*: https://www.moma.org/explore/inside_out/2010/04/05/100-years-a-history-of-performance-art/?high_contrast=true.

4. Bishop, Claire, *Antagonism and Relational Aesthetics*, October, N.110, Autumn 2004, pp.51-80; Bishop, Op. Cit., 2006.

5. Bloom, Harold, *The Anxiety of Influence. A Theory of Poetry*, Oxford University Press, New York, 1973.

6. Gilbert, Sandra and Gubar, Susan, *The Madwoman in the Attic. The Woman Writer and the Nineteenth-Century Literary Imagination*, Yale University Press, Yale, 1979.

7. Gilbert and Gubar, *ibid*. p.59.

8. Haraway, Donna, *Conocimientos situados: la cuestión científica en el feminismo y el privilegio de la perspectiva parcial*, in *Ciencia, cyborgs y mujeres. La reinvención de la naturaleza*, Cátedra, Madrid, 1995, p.328.

9. We should bear in mind, however, that collaborative art practices and the community arts have aroused interest from policy-makers seeking to use culture as a means of social management, and from arts funding sources needing to enhance their legitimacy through a commitment to social welfare. See Yúdice, George, *El recurso de la cultura. Usos de la cultura en la era global*, Gedisa, Barcelona, 2002.

10. Cottingham, Laura, *Not For Sale: Feminism and Art in the USA during the 1970s*, video recording, 87'40", 1998.

11. Cottingham, Laura, *On the Making of Not For Sale, Apexart*, 1998, https://apexart.org/exhibitions/cottingham.php, accessed 12th March 2018.

12. *Prácticas da História*, No.3, Special Issue: *The Archive and the Subaltern*, 2016 (http://www.praticasdahistoria.pt/en/issues/praticas-da-historia-no-3-2016); Eichhorn, Kate, *The Archival Turn in Feminism. Outrage in Order*, Temple University Press, Philadelphia, PA, 2013.

13. Sangster, Joan, *Telling our stories: feminist debates and the use of oral history* in *Women's History Review*, 3:1, 1994, pp.5-28; Steyerl, Hito, *Can Witnesses Speak? On the Philosophy of the Interview* in *European Institute for Progressive Cultural Policies*, 2008, http://eipcp.net/transversal/0408/steyerl/en, accessed 21st February 2018,

14. Burke, Peter, *Obertura: la nueva historia, su pasado y su futuro* in *Formas de hacer historia*, Alianza Universidad, Madrid, 1994, pp.11-37.

15. Harding, Anna (ed.), *Magic Moments: Collaborations Between Artists and Young People*, Black Dog Publishing, London, 2006.

16. Neue Gesellschaft für bildene Kunst, *Art For Change. Lorraine Leeson. Works from 1975-2005/Arbeiten von 1975 bis 2005*, Neue Gesellschaft für Bildende Kunst, Berlin, 2005.

17. http://transductores.info

18. Vagabond Reviews, *More Bite in the Real World: Usership in Arts-Based Research Practice* in Birchall, M, and Sack, M, (eds.) *After the Turn: Art Education beyond the Museum. Vol.24 Zurich: On Curating*, 2014 pp.

Where values emerge: an in-depth exploration of the Collaborative Arts Partnership Programme's process, discoveries and learning

Susanne Bosch

Introduction

This essay, *Where values emerge*, will draw on four years of research within the Collaborative Arts Partnership Programme (CAPP). It will give an overview of the values that have proved to be essential to the CAPP process, and how these developed over the four years of the programme. My role at CAPP as artist researcher was very much embedded. I facilitated elements of partner meetings, and I conducted sessions with all the partners; transcripts of some of these will be made available in the CAPP resources online.[1] I interviewed staff, artists, participants and collaborators. Research within CAPP engaged with a critical analysis of socially engaged, collaborative artistic practices from different perspectives – institutions, co-producers and artists – aiming to contribute to better practice and better policy-making.

CAPP as a network understood 'collaboration' to be a rich body of economic, ecological, societal, cultural and ethical attitudes and qualities. CAPP looked at how collaboration in the contemporary world can help us to rethink human interaction and societal order. In the light of massive global changes between 2014-18 (e.g. Brexit and the refugee crisis), the CAPP partners constructed and deconstructed narratives of collaboration, which I will discuss in this essay, focusing on the values that underpin such collaboration.

CAPP's objectives, activities and expectations were defined by all partners involved, and the process was given rhythm by regular meetings. The choice of sites and collaborative art approaches by the nine CAPP partners was crucial, and led to a number of new formats, new institutional structures and new concepts. CAPP was an invitation to explore collaboration in, with and about the arts, offering new understandings inspired by collaborative values. Collaborative arts is often stigmatised as being worth less than 'high art', more so in some countries than others. Collaborative arts is also often commodified at the expense of its intrinsic value.

What does collaboration mean in this context?

Patrick Fox, Director of Heart of Glass (formerly Director of Create), explained the genesis of the CAPP project: "We looked at what could be done within the Creative Europe Scheme. We began a process with a smaller group of partners (Tate Liverpool, Live Art Development Agency and m-cult), and we explored what the professional development needs of artists who work collaboratively might be, and where the gaps lay. This was conducted in 2014, and involved various strands of dialogue, including a survey completed by artists. We also hosted a summit, the European Learning Network gathering in Dublin, which convened artists, and saw those in the room co-create a roadmap for what a co-operation project might look like. What came back strongly included opportunities to network with peers as well as professional development, exchange and increased commission opportunities."

Working together is a big focus in industry, politics and other sector networks, because an increasingly mobile and diverse culture needs an understanding of common ground. According to Mark Terkessidis, collaboration is different from co-operation, as co-operating partners diverge when their joint activity is finished.[2] Collaboration promotes a form of working where the process will change all involved members, and the collaborators welcome this change. Collaboration is not an unstructured process, but rather is goal-oriented and practical. Authority is not neglected, but rather is shaped by working together. Sometimes the process is more crucial than its result: collaboration deals with complexity and

contradictions, and tries to develop pragmatic frameworks. Collaboration is more of a life practice than a solely artistic method.

In the arts, the term 'collaborative practice' has been common since the 1960s. Recently, 'participatory' and 'collaborative' have been used for all kinds of activities and audience involvement. Often, funding schemes lead to projects where collaboration does not go beyond including participants in an aesthetic dimension of a work.

The discourse on collaboration and collectivity is noticeably critical within the arts. This critique and even rejection can be traced back several years. In the aftermath of Nicolas Bourriaud's publication *Relational Aesthetics*, which described participation and interaction as a central paradigm of contemporary art, critics took note of the democratisation promised by participation and collaboration.[3] Claire Bishop notes, in her widely acclaimed essay *Antagonism and Relational Aesthetics*, that most projects create the impression of idyllic "togetherness" rather than exposing the complex and potentially antagonistic dynamics of democratic collaborations.[4] Bishop describes the climax of the discourse as an "ethical turn" in criticism.[5] Generally speaking, the ethical concerns are based on a scepticism that artists only allow pseudo-participation, but actually implement their own ideas while relying on other – mostly non-art – people to realise the artwork. In this case, "collaborative" art is merely an artistic reproduction of power practices, concealed by the impression of "togetherness".

There is, without doubt, a hierarchy in collaborative art projects. Collaboration does not mean self-abandonment for the artist (or any involved art institution), nor a complete loss of control. The artist has a defined authority through their ideas, knowledge, ways of expression, networks, profile and often paid time. What needs to be decided jointly is how they will work with their non-artist collaborators, and what the expectations are. This is something that CAPP explored in all of its projects, and which I will discuss here.

Narratives from co-producers

The quotes from co-producers throughout this essay are from events and partner meetings, as well as interviews with artists, partners, producers and participants. They are partly set up to challenge perceptions about collaborative arts in the framework of hierarchical structures. The findings expressed are deliberately provocative, in an attempt to widen horizons on collaborative art practices

as the common definition of narratives is based on supposed consensus.

Collaborative arts practice is reflexive, in that it learns from its own processes and participants, and feeds back into the work as it develops. CAPP, as an accumulation of artists, institutions and partners with artistic, theoretical, sociological or architectural backgrounds, explored various ways of being creative and then reflexive.

Value one: taking care of the organisational matrix

The CAPP network, as it called itself a "collaborative arts partnership programme", had to intend to be collaborative to be truthful to its own objectives.

The initial role of the lead partner, Create, was to create opportunities for the institutions to exchange experiences, to invite and test these complex collaborative processes in their local context, and to nurture their own talents as part of a wider practice. Partner meetings and online exchanges worked as invitations to witness each other's processes. As host, Create needed to secure the quality of this complex and sensitive process by inspiring and creating opportunities, and by initially setting the tone through the way everyone was invited, how the process was facilitated and how the environment was taken account of.

There were two to three partner meetings a year in different locations throughout Europe. From 2016, meetings included public moments known as Staging Posts. CAPP Staging Posts were opportunities to reflect on the various projects that had taken place across the CAPP territories throughout the four year arc. There were also opportunities to discuss wider issues in relation to collaborative ways of working, public engagement and social responsibility. Specific topics highlighted the CAPP network's challenges, including agency in Helsinki, language in Osnabrück, practice/participation/politics in London and innovative formats of knowledge exchange in St. Helens.[6]

In the project set up phase, Patrick Fox and Lynnette Moran, both former members of the Create team, asked colleagues a set of core questions in 2014 to start a co-creation process. The collective meaning making would develop a multi-perspective view of our field with the idea of having deeper insights into our systems and creating new actions.

The practice-based learning was written into a project proposal which acted as a guide over the four years of CAPP. The *how* would be decided by the process and how it was designed. From the outset, there were questions of self-organisation and sustainable structures beyond the period of four years. A noticeable change occurred in October 2016: the CAPP institutions decided jointly that they had learned to work with each other and had developed enough trust to divide up into sub groups with responsibility for events, for supporting the research process and for publications and finance. At this point, the CAPP process started to unfold with a more long-term intention. It opened up to a wider community of practitioners in the form of Staging Posts, an active web presence, publications and presentations at other events.

Commenting on how the internal processes of CAPP have worked, Sören Meschede from hablarenarte said: "With our Spanish partners, we wanted to create a network but there was no energy, time or interest from those responsible to really engage in such a dialogue. It led to us having one to one conversations with everyone, but with no communication between our four Spanish partners. We realised our intended structures would never work. You cannot discuss many things on an individual, one to one basis. For example, should we set up an open call for a particular CAPP opportunity and if so how? Discussing proceedings is complicated. It seems impossible to create long-term collaborations

if people are not in the room together. People work very well when they are together, but when back in their own organisation it overwhelms them. I really think group communication is difficult to maintain and manage, especially amongst institutions. One to one is easier. It comes down to lack of time and that is connected to resources."[7]

Value two: taking hosting seriously – making a shared space with diverse others

Hosting is a form of taking matters into our own, self-organised hands, to allow innovation to happen beyond control and top-down expertise. This type of co-intelligence arrives at the creative border between chaos and order. Hosting is the idea of opening, holding and sharing a space with diverse others. For that to take place, people being present in a space is the starting point for joint encounters. There needs to be an understanding of interdependence, with an atmosphere of trust, respect, care, appreciation, listening and interest. Changing formats of hosting and exchange with others allowed for different encounters within the CAPP network. Critical friend Herman Bashiron Mendolicchio noted about his CAPP experiences: "After a quite intense stay in Liverpool and St. Helens there are many things to think about, some

contradictions... the intensity of collaboration, but at the same time the feeling of lack of being hosted... Observing and experiencing different CAPP events (from inside and from outside) is very nourishing."[8]

Value three: the importance of partnership and friendship

CAPP's approach considered how to build a relational arts practice based on mutual respect, partnership and friendship, recognising that communication and dialogue are an integral part of successful co-operation. Grant Kester suggests that the particular quality of collaborative art is based on the quality of relationships between all collaborators, which is borne out by the CAPP process.[9]

According to Gesa Ziemer, self-organisation within the arts works because of the integration of the Other.[10] When we refer to a relational art practice that is based on mutual respect, trust, partnership and friendship, Derrida's understanding of friendship might help to identify the qualities of such relations: Derrida emphasises that friendly co-operation or the concept of friendship itself is aimed at the integration of the Other, and thus aimed at at a dialogue with and between many different things. *Public Address Systems* by Lois Weaver[11] and generative dialogue developed by quantum physicist David Bohm,[12] are two examples of tried and tested formats that involve many different people, and thus avoid the predominant approach of individual competition. These dialogical processes shape the negotiation of involved power and decision-making consciously through their form.

Artist and activist John Jordan argues that "... at the root of what we do is radical friendship. We create these tools, these actions and these moments, but because we work horizontally, we try to work with a collective spirit. The key is creating friendships. We think the basics of any politics is the trust, the friendship and the love that is created through these intense moments of working together in disobedience."[13] These kinds of relationships are crucial to the collaboration that CAPP fosters. As hablarenarte summarised: "The goal is to create a trusting environment so that people begin to propose things, to contradict, and to question. That is when a collective or collaborative process can truly begin."[14]

Value four: allowing participants to maintain personal agency

Jordan speaks as an artist and activist about the attitude needed to establish trusting relationships. Projects within the CAPP network experienced a series of challenges for the co-producer units, such as being invited into complex contexts, sometimes by more than one partner with different expectations, under specific conditions of time and finance. Conflict negotiation and a constant flow of communication was necessary to find common ground, and to clarify different expectations and needs. Through regular reflections at partner meetings, the CAPP partners recognised challenges and conflict as a learning opportunity and indicator of change.

The Convivialist Manifesto declares: "Conflict is a necessary and natural part of every society, not only because interests and opinions constantly differ, but also because every human being aspires to have their uniqueness recognized and this results in an element of rivalry as powerful and primordial as the aspiration, also common to all, to harmony and co-operation... In short, we have to make conflict a force for life rather than a force for death. And we have to turn rivalry into a means of co-operation, a weapon with which to ward off violence and the destruction it entrains."[15]

Given the intensely collaborative nature of CAPP as a whole, it is not surprising that the Staging Post in Helsinki addressed 'shades of agency' as its leading topic.[16] At the current stage of collaborative practices, how partners and projects deal with difficult situations and how they narrate the solutions and approaches to the wider field, is a key issue.

Dublin-based artist Michelle Browne addressed the idea of 'reputational economy' in a session in Helsinki, about the dilemmas that might face partners and artists: "You try your best to work horizontally but then someone will make you the leader, as you are the brand that can be plastered onto that work."[17] Browne echoes what artist María Ruido states in her interview with hablarenarte, that this type of "collaboration is proposed from the artist's perspective" and sits still within the artistic context of uniqueness and promotion of individuals.[18] Within collaborative art practices these affiliations disturb, as the initiator of collaboration must be capable of fostering trust and interest within co-producer units and of guiding the process.

Value five: committing to honest and collaborative relationship(s)

I have highlighted the scale and depth of importance that relationships play in this field. CAPP members often mentioned struggling to find the correct terminology for the qualities we try to address in the programme. I refer to co-producer units; what makes these distinct from other work or project forces is the need of the unit to commit to other people, often strangers, in a jointly agreed process.

Commitment is one of the most important topics within this field of practice and was also the issue that co-producer units found the most difficult to talk about, as commitments are understood very differently. As described by Terkessidis, deciding how to work together, and what mutual expectations are, is a delicate task. Work that is committed to social ethics in a globally tense situation might work against the demands of the art itself.

Furthermore, ego-driven attitudes of co-producer unit members can endanger delicate relational work. Honest and open communication is needed. That means that the relationship between institutions and artists has to be right and the intention clear: who is hosting the artist, the process and the community in order to create a meaningful contribution? Clarification of expectations and the nature of invitation is a must, in order for all parties to commit to the process in a meaningful way.

Partners should be equally matched in terms of speed of working, the involved wo/manpower, flexibility and institutional hierarchies, as well as forms of decision-making. In order for collaborations to work fluently and well, the entire co-producer unit needs to define the work and be realistic about the scale of the work. In short, this type of practice demands a mature attitude to negotiate the contradictions between neo-liberal, competitive settings and the demands of interdependent and interconnected work. Consequently, one needs to create locally adapted cultures based on already existing resources and intelligence. In all of this, the expectation of a return in the form of professional, economic or market recognition is not necessarily a given.

Speaking about committing to relationships emotionally, Patrick Fox from Heart of Glass said: "We need to know our personal limits. We are in an insane moment in global politics... how far will we go for our beliefs and what are our limits? I do not know what my personal answer for that is, but I need to know organisationally because every project we do speaks to some democratic crisis, or has a explicit or implicit political emphasis. What does that mean for an organisation? We have to author our own limits. Already, as we receive public funding, we are complicit within a structure because we take the money, we report data, we are part of the structure of the system. The external environment is changing. It is a lot about life and death, now. The infrastructure is the same but I think the art world is not grasping the severity of the social and political situation. We do not have the luxury to make work in a voyeuristic way, to present a work *about* something – the work needs to be more active."[19]

Value six: seeing time as currency – being slow, doing less?

Time is the invisible material of relational work. Artists often report a lack of adequate process time, to the extent that one's own body, finances and family are neglected out of loyalty to the artistic process.

David Beech highlights how "durational work has become exemplary of a certain strain of discourse which calls for an ethical foundation for the relationships developed between an artist and a community."[20] He identifies the discourse of duration as ideological, highlighting Thomas Crow's suspicion of "duration as a sign of the failure to engage seriously with the contradictions of social space". The amount of time spent with the community is read as a sign of quality, charging artists and curators "with having pastoral care over their publics."[21]

While Crow focuses on the physical conception of site, art historian Miwon Kwon's understanding of site is expanded to the social, economic and political sphere. Kwon demands an artist be sensitive to specificities of site. What gives "ongoing invented communities" their sustainability, according to Kwon, is "the artists' intimate and direct knowledge of their respective neighbourhoods."[22]

Time spent on art processes is problematised by being linked to political and economic debates; Beech suggests moving away from the oppositional binary of not enough or too much time, instead thinking about quality.[23] I welcome his suggestion, but I feel that the time for art needs to be made consciously by all parties.

When looking at the timeframes that CAPP projects offered, they did not differ much from other invites or open calls. Many I spoke with mentioned the challenge of giving themselves permission to slow down. We argue in the field that we do not know how to work more slowly and we do not dare to do it for multiple reasons: funders' expectations of quantity, the pressure of a CV, the fear of being left behind. We also face the reality that participants do not value the time an art project might take. Children and young people, for example, were often too busy with school and after school activities to commit to longer projects.

Kelly Green, residency artist at LADA, speaks about how time can be further problematised by other unexpected occasions as well as long-term external commitments – in her case, a practice-based PhD and motherhood. "It was full on and pretty great, but hard. I was meant to make a toolkit and study guide at the end, but now, as my computer crashed, I am behind on that. I have to go to Wales this week and I am a single mum. I think I stretched myself too thin: as a woman, as a single mum from a working class background, I've got to prove myself all the time. By saying I need support, that makes me quite vulnerable. What I learned with this project is that I need to be clearer on those boundaries to be realistic what is un/doable. I think this project could have needed a co-ordinator and someone on communication; it took a lot of time with all these different partners involved and three locations, two exhibitions, etc., but to demand something makes me feel uncomfortable. It is hard for a single mum to get involved in institutions because of their unsociable hours. My mum agreed to watch my child so I could work long hours and do the travel to Canterbury and Wales. That was all amazing for me as I cannot not do it usually. With a bit of distance you know it is not doable with these resources, to do it really well and you see yourself that you do lots of stuff not well, and it is not how you want to do it."[24]

CAPP often failed to address foreseeable challenges such as art-typical timeframes and being able to commit enough time for the negotiation process, as well as unexpected situations and the expected messiness of collaborative processes. Meschede named the lack of time as most common reason for a non-committed team of collaborators.[25] But CAPP also experimented successfully with new time formats, e.g. by Heart of Glass and artist Mark Storor initiating a 12-year residency. Such duration, based on the content of the work, must be read as a provocation to the entire structure of art commissions and residencies. Rejecting the monumental, this art genre focuses not primarily on the quality of the object but on the quality of the temporal experience the project offers to a group of people.

Collaboration fails when time is ignored or handled as it would be in other art projects. Glenn Loughran and Lindsey Fryer refer to inefficiency as the very nature of the work. Fryer says: "This practice takes a lot more investment of time across the whole organisation than the traditional exhibition format. For example, if you commission an artist to do an exhibition it might cost £10,000 including the artists' fee. These collaborative commissions can cost between £40-50,000. You need to support the artist over an extended period of research time building relationships with local people. And when you're working with communities you have to support them with travel and food. You don't have to do that with an artist making an installation, for example. That is why the commissioning organisation has to change significantly to support this developmental way of working. Marketing deadlines need to be stretched, using social media and digital formats more creatively and openly. Expecting a title and project information in the usual time scale is unrealistic, as these works are often shaped by the process of working with others. Challenging the normal institutional process needs staff to be creative flexible, adaptable and resourceful. Understanding this contemporary practice across the organisation is vital for organisational change and development. For *Art Gym*, co-curated with young people in Tate Collective, we needed to listen, to understand what young people need, and to learn from them rather than imposing impossible systems and structures onto them. *Art Gym* achieved 10,200 participants/visitors in three weeks. This is far more than traditional exhibitions over the same period, and far more impactful on young people delivering it and those visiting with family and friends. So there needs to be a major shift in how the institution brings collaborative practice into the programme, how it is resourced and how staff understand the practice and its impact on communities. Learning from our CAPP programme, we have a further three years of collaborative practice projects planned and we are making progress within the institution, we are making a difference and there are signs of getting there."[26]

Valentina Karga, residency artist with m-cult, discussed how she makes time for herself within her own practice. Karga uses meditation as part of her practice, and did yoga every morning as part of her residency. Karga explains: "It's my constant. When you travel so much I think it's good to have some consistency because the context changes so much. So you have to find a constant and the most reliable constant is yourself. Actually there is nothing else... the body is very important in this equation because how you feel is immediately communicated in your body. So if your body is tense then that also makes you feel tense, and think in a tensed way. I make space very deliberately for this. I take it. Even when I feel like I don't have time. When the mind tells you, you don't have time for this and that, but I really just go ahead and do it."[27]

In a conversation with Oskia Ugarte, one of the four directors of Centro Huarte in Pamplona and Georg Zolchow from hablarenarte Madrid, time was identified as an issue, both in terms of accessing sufficient time for exchange and reflection and in terms of being recognised as a resource, as a currency within a collaborative process. For Ugarte, finding time to inform the work was the challenge, not so much organising project working times among a collaborative team of four directors.

For Zolchow it was very much about time to reflect: "We [hablarenarte] lack time to meet and talk. And that impacts on the quality of work and quality of relationships. This year was terrible in that sense. We sometimes do not see each other for two weeks. And then we have so much to talk about that we do not find the four hours that we would need. To sit and talk and think together is fundamental for projects like this one. If we do not have the time, these projects fail."

These conversations revealed a strong sense of the need to value relational time, and to make very deliberate decisions to create the conditions for nurturing that. In reflecting on how that might happen, Zolchow observed: "It is more complex. To slow things down is an answer. I do not know how to do it. We all agree on that in the cultural sector but we do not know how to do it, none of us. In a European project, time is measured against money." [28]

It seems essential that the slower, non-activity-filled relational time is established from within the field or project itself. And it seems important that it is established by those who understand the importance of and value of this type of non-action time, for the quality of the process, the outcome and the resilience of the entire setting.

Value seven: allowing 'inefficiency' – fighting for long lasting activities and against burn out.

When considering efficiency, the collective La Fundició demand a paradigm shift: "If we were to stop seeing ourselves as something separate from the situations and processes of collective creation, to stop trying to control them from a privileged position and by means of external calculation, then it would no longer be possible to measure their 'effectiveness' in terms of the degree to which objectives are attained, and they would no longer fall within the dialectic between success and failure."[29]

Artist and educator Glenn Loughran similarly highlights efficiency-thinking as an embedded, reductive set of neo-liberal prescriptions: "Socially engaged art is an absolutely cumbersome, inefficient way to work because you are at the mercy of deep processes that can go either way. We can develop skills to make that better, but it can never be a totally efficient process, and it shouldn't be; when it's efficient it's questionable."[30]

The term 'inefficiency' in relation to collaborative arts practice creates interesting thought processes. If the nature of this practice is being qualified as inefficient, the idea of a quick fix through this type of art is not suitable. Non-art-based co-producers are often the most vital in these projects, and they are often the most unheard. They are 'inefficient', difficult, unwilling at times to be involved in devising the structure of a project, because they follow the natural logic of a process, not so much a project plan. CAPP projects realised that institutions need to put themselves into the non-art-based co-producer structures rather than the reverse.

Collaborative practices and processes are complex and messy, and (often) fun. Co-producer units and/or individuals take knowledge and then try to apply it to their situation. This results in locally adapted cultures based on local resources, local intelligence and local work.

Artist Mark Storor was one of the most creative people in introducing me to the paradigm of inefficiency in our field: he dealt with me, the researcher, by inviting me to witness his making rather than talking about it. Storor moved to St Helens in 2016, but was commissioned in Rhyl and invited me to witness his working methods there.[31]

His decision to spend his time making – and not talking – demanded flexibility from me. How are artists contributing to particular places

over time? I talked to a lady who took part in his project and played a key role within the town. I learned about his practice through others talking about it. Storor puts 100% of his attention towards to other people and their potential. His attention to others and his way of engaging aesthetically as well as socially travel ahead of him. As he does not believe in language being strong enough to translate the value of his work, he invited me to be a witness. This approach draws attention to the value and importance of observation as a way to understand practice, rather than verbal exchange.

Value eight: encouraging a more care-based artistic practice: the gift as methodology

Through the CAPP process, I have spent a lot of time thinking about what collaborative art practices are giving to the world. Why do I speak of a 'gift', when looking at a co-producer-unit creating change through an artistic practice? Why is the term 'gift' useful in the context of collaborative arts practices, instead of speaking of a transaction? What does it mean to let go of the idea of growth as guarantor for happiness and wealth? We need a new social, moral and political philosophy for living together, since democracy and ecological survival cannot rely any longer on the idea of infinite economic growth.

Thus, we have to oppose the global hegemony of finance capitalism and look for forms of prosperity without growth. *Conviviality* is the term introduced by Ivan Illich to express the "art of living together."[32] In 2014, in *Convivialist Manifesto: A declaration of interdependence*, 40 French-speaking individuals wrote a manifesto for a constructive solution to today's world: "The prime concern [...] is the quality of our social relationships [...] The term [convivialism] is meant to point out the fact that the main task we face is that of working out a new philosophy and developing practical forms of peaceful interaction."[33] The point for Illich was to restore the primacy of 'being' over 'having', by exposing the flaws in technology and capitalism.

Care and gift are the immediate translation into action of the interdependence that characterises the whole of humankind, and which has been integral to CAPP. "Societies reproduce themselves symbolically and socially via a cycle of giving, receiving, and reciprocating. What [ethnographer Marcel] Mauss[34] was concerned with was a third principle – namely, 'solidarity' as a form of mutual recognition secured by the exchange of gifts founded on social ties and mutual endebtedness."[35] This 'third way', solidarity, beyond the purported absolutes of state and market, is one of the key political demands of the MAUSS movement.[36]

The CAPP experiences name the complexity of gifts exchanged. This type of art practice often focused on finding common ground, and pooling resources, knowledge and activities for purposes that do not lie primarily in the making of profit. CAPP projects were challenged to find creative answers while facing contemporary crises that affected the projects.

Sophie Mahon, residency artist with Heart of Glass, speaks about the importance of being able to explore artistically without pressure over outcomes – a shift away from the normal pressures put in place by funders and employers. She says: "I love Heart of Glass, as it is all about the process. They never asked me once about the outcome as such. They have always been: how is it working with that person? How are the ideas developing? I applied for an open call because I am interested in northern towns like these, in a lot of ways it's similar to my own home, a deprived post industrial town. When I read the brief, I thought, I can do that because I have been that young person. I can give these young people a voice as where I come from is not a million miles away."[37] She further describes how this work with Heart of Glass allowed her to establish a relationship with young people who slowly responded to the cycle of her giving, by receiving and reciprocating.

Jakob and Manila Bartnik, a collaborative artist couple in Osnabrück, Germany, regularly work with the gift as methodology to invite people into the exchange cycle. Antje Schiffers, a German artist, collaborated in 2017 with Museum Ludwig in Budapest and the curator Katalin Erdődi. In her ongoing work, *I like being a farmer and I would like to stay one*, there is a reciprocal exchange between herself and a farmer family. She works for a week on a farm, painting outdoors, while asking the family to document their reality on video as well as hosting her.

Value nine: finding a strategic balance between form and content, approach and ethics

"Politics is not solely, or even primarily, about reasoned thinking and rational choices; it's an affair of fantasy and desire. People are rarely moved to action, support, or even consent by realistic proposals; they are motivated by dreams of what could be."[38]

The institutional formats within CAPP differ greatly in scale and mission. Institutions on the edges of the art market offer the most flexibility and therefore the most potential in the eco-system of art. Collaborative arts practices are often not clearly positioned, and sit between fields of art, education, activism, ethnography research and other related fields. Being dependent and embedded mainly in the artistic field creates tensions. There is a demand to produce excellent contemporary art when working with cultural institutions. 'Excellent' here means responding to the aesthetic language of the hosting institution in one way or the other. Often, this does not match with the approach, content, ethics or skills of the collaborative project. On the other hand, artists are often obsessed by the aesthetic form so that they tend to neglect the political narrative behind it. If the two are not interlinked with the project aims, the work becomes pointless. The challenge is to find a balance between urgency and necessity in order to create maximum attention for the project.[39]

Minna Tarkka from m-cult reflects on their strategy of working with artists on projects that combine media art and collaboration, in the neighbourhood of Maunula in Helsinki: "We learned that some artists needed support for media art techniques, and some for the social collaboration. The need for support arises from the hybrid nature of the artists' practice. For example, Valentina Karga made this totem and a video-manifesto representing the values of the future community. In her interview, she says she wants to be an amateur. It was interesting to see how the curator, producer and co-producer can support the artist in opening new paths for their work. We worked a lot on the ground in the neighbourhood and wanted to smooth the way. It was not just translation of language, it was a translation of the concept of the artist that we were trying to do."[40]

Conclusion

CAPP explored collaborative arts practices in order to develop new forms of representation for the field. Within the practices, CAPP found that the values important for human togetherness are also important within collaborative arts projects. How can we consider values and qualities of collaboration in the arts in a contemporary setting of social transformation? How can we uncover values in an age of growing cultural, economic and political uncertainty, in a neo-liberal environment of competitiveness? In order to share its richness, the cultural field needs to renew its understanding of collaboration in order to set up a more suitable language, financial and other structures, such as decision-making, timeframes and forms of learning.

How can CAPP 'seed' wisdom differently? How can we fertilise new grounds for human togetherness through artistic practice? More importantly, we need to think about possible futures that may emerge from such practices: futures involving an altered way of speaking, thinking and doing. With the following provocations, I would like to summarise where the CAPP network had deeper insights into the values and qualities of collaboration in, with and through the arts. Collaborative values of human togetherness emerge:

- when accepting inefficiency. 'Inefficiency' is the nature of this practice in a neo-liberal environment. The shift happens when slowing down to make work.

- when accepting the power of 'bottom up': the co-producers, initially called participants, are the movers and shakers, but at the same time they are the most unheard voice. It is even more 'inefficient' to get them structurally involved. Therefore artistic institutions need to work to bring participants or co-producers into *their* structures, or adapt to the co-producers' structures themselves.

- when the friendly chemistry between institutions, artists and the entire co-producer-unit is working well and the process is hosted properly.

- when we understand the importance of radical relational approaches for this type of work: ego-driven attitudes slow down the flow and endanger relational work. An honest, open way of speaking is needed between all involved to create a resilient and substantial piece of work. The clarification of professional expectations within the co-producer unit is a must.

- when understanding the direction of the work: mature co-producer units have a lot to share in terms of their attitude, approaches and methodologies, such as the focus on care/self-care, and the need for conscious and self-reflective action, courage and taking risks.

- when being clear that collaborative art is a life practice, not solely an artistic practice. There is no division between the two.

Currently, the world experiences political leadership performed by popular heroes or tycoon-type characters who base their legitimation on radical self-empowerment. Democratic culture based on acknowledging human interconnectedness on a local, regional and international scale is slowly vanishing. Furthermore, attitudes are changing fast when it comes to dealing with contested societal contexts in a political way, which often entails decisions that ignore important aspects, postpone finding sustainable solutions and creates stress for the parties involved.

In 2015, Frederica Thieme from Art Way Of Thinking opened her workshop with the CAPP network by congratulating all of us on work that matters greatly and pointing out how, even within very challenging conditions, collaborative art practices can make constructive contributions to peaceful coexistence in a contemporary setting of global, cultural and social transformation. The process of negotiating our difficulties and highlighting the values created in this field of work will continue.

Dr. Susanne Bosch is an artist and independent researcher.

Endnotes

1. See www.cappnetwork.com [accessed 19th April 2018]

2. Terkessidis, Mark, *Kollaboration*, edition Suhrkamp, Berlin, 2015

3. Bourriaud, Nicolas, *Relational Aesthetics*, Les presses du réel, Dijon, 2002

4. Bishop, Claire, *Antagonism and Relational Aesthetics* in *October Magazine*, Massachusetts Institute of Technology, No 110 (Fall 2004)

5. Bishop, Claire, *The Social Turn, Collaboration and Its Discontents*, in Schavemaker, Margriet and Rakier, Mischa (eds), in *Right About Now: Art and Theory Since the 1990s*, Valiz, Amsterdam, 2007

6. See www.cappnetwork.com [accessed 19th April 2018]

7. Sören Meschede in conversation with Susanne Bosch, Madrid, June 2017

8. Herman Bashiron Mendolicchio, from an e-mail to Susanne Bosch, 24th April 2018

9. Kester, Grant, *Conversation Pieces: Community and Communication in Modern Art*, University of California Press, Los Angeles, 2004

10. Ziemer, Gesa, *Konvivialistische Kunst? Über das freundschaftliche Zusammenleben im urbanen Raum*. In: Frank Adloff, Volker M. Heins (Hg.) Konvivialismus. *Eine Debatte*. Transcript Verlag, Bielefeld, 2015, p 182

11. www.split-britches.com/publicaddresssystems [accessed 15th December 2017]

12. sprott.physics.wisc.edu/Chaos-Complexity/dialogue.pdf [accessed 11th December 2017]

13. John Jordan on Creative Activism, www.youtube.com/watch?v=WPQ2MyLwiJI [accessed 11th December 2017]

14. *Impossible Glossary*, published by hablarenarte, p.13, www.hablarenarte.com/en/proyecto/id/capp-impossible-glossary [accessed 11th March 2018]

15. 15th June 2017, www.cappnetwork.com/capp-event/shades-of-agency/ [accessed 11th December 2017]

16. *Convivialist Manifesto. A declaration of interdependence (Global Dialogues 3)*, with an introduction by Frank Adloff, translated from the French by Margaret Clarke. Duisburg 2014: Käte Hamburger Kolleg / Centre for Global Cooperation. Originally published in French as *MANIFESTE CONVIVIALISTE. Déclaration d'interdépendance*, Éditions Le Bord de L'Eau 2013

17. Dilemma session initiated and lead by artist Tellervo Kalleinen, 15th June 2017, www.cappnetwork.com/capp-event/shades-of-agency/

18. *Impossible Glossary*, published by hablarenarte, p.14, www.hablarenarte.com/en/proyecto/id/capp-impossible-glossary [accessed 11th March 2018]

19. Patrick Fox in conversation with Susanne Bosch, March 2017

20. Beech, David, *The Ideology of Duration in the Dematerialised Monument: Art, Sites, Publics and Time* in Doherty, Claire and O'Neil, Paul (eds), *Locating the Producers: Durational Approaches to Public Art*, Valiz, Amsterdam, 2009, p. 314

21. Beech, *ibid*, p. 318

22. Kwon, p. 134 in Beech, *ibid*, p.324

23. Such as "delay, interruption, stages, flows, of instantaneous performances and lingering documents, of temporary objects and permanent mementos, of repetition, echo and seriality", Beech, *ibid*, p. 325

24. Kelly Green in conversation with Susanne Bosch, March 2017

25. Lindsey Fryer in conversation with Susanne Bosch, June 2017

26. Sören Meschede in conversation with Susanne Bosch, March 2017

27. Valentina Karga in conversation with Susanne Bosch, October 2017

28. Oskia Ugarte and Georg Zolchow in conversation with Susanne Bosch, June 2017

29. *Impossible Glossary*, published by hablarenarte, p.144, www.hablarenarte.com/en/proyecto/id/capp-impossible-glossary [online 11th March 2018]

30. In conversation with Susanne Bosch in February 2017

31. Drawing upon Rhyl and its people for inspiration, *Lifted by Beauty: Adventures in Dreaming* was both produced and performed collaboratively in spring 2018. www.nationaltheatrewales.org/lifted-beauty [accessed 17th January 2018]

32. Illich, Ivan, *Tools for Conviviality*, New York, NY: Harper & Row, 1973

33. Text excerpt from *Convivialism Transnational*, written by Frank Adloff, convivialism.org/ [accessed 17th January 2018]

34. Mauss, Marcel, *The Gift. The Form and Reason for Exchange in Archaic Societies*, New York, NY: W. W. Norton, 1924

35. dialoguesenhumanite.org/sites/dialoguesenhumanite.org/files/meetuppage/103/convivialist-manifesto.pdf [accessed 17th January 2018] p.11

36. 'Mouvement Anti-Utilitariste dans les Sciences Socialies' – Anti-Utilitarian Movement in Social Sciences

37. Sophie Mahon in conversation with Susanne Bosch, March 2017

38. From Stephen Duncombe, *Dream: Re-imagining Progressive Politics in an Age of Fantasy*, 2008, www.stephenduncombe.com/dreampolitik/ [accessed 11th December 2017]

39. John Jordan on Creative Activism, www.youtube.com/watch?v=WPQ2MyLwiJI [accessed 11th December 2017]

40. CAPP partners Poarch talk on residencies in London, March 2017

DIALOGUES

Practice

The dialogue on practice is structured as four interviews with participants of CAPP projects about their impressions of being part of a collaboration. The format for this dialogue was devised by Sören Meschede, hablarenarte.

MANTA - Art, Fight and Learning is a project with Alexander Ríos and Byron Maher, along with the Union of Street Sellers and Can Collectors that asks if art can contribute to marginalised or disadvantaged social contexts? And if so, in which ways?

The conversation about MANTA took place in March 2018 in Madrid between Malick Gueye and Ndir El Hadji Sec, both members of the Madrid Union of Street Sellers and Can Collectors.

The conversation was conducted in Woloff dialect, translated to Spanish and then to English.

Would you please briefly describe the project?
The project consists of showing the Union of Street Sellers and Can Collectors' struggle to find collective alternatives to social and institutional racism – using art to bring visibility to the exclusion and problems suffered by our collective.

Why did you join this project?
Because I believe collective struggle is the only way to combat discrimination. Our Union is made up of people of different nationalities, and we have come together to organise collectively and fight for a change. We are street sellers because as non-documented immigrants there are so many barriers for us to legally earn our living. The art project allows us to make this visible in a different and more powerful way.

Briefly describe your role in the project.
I have played the same role as any other member of the collective: contributing my efforts, taking part in decision-making and sharing my desire to change things.

www.cappnetwork.com/capp-project/
social-element/

For you, what does it mean to be an artist?
Being an artist is a way of perceiving reality
that allows us to observe and analyse to create
a different way of showing the needs and
problems of the world. An artist has tools that
can help to spread our message.

Who are Alex and Byron for you?
First and foremost, they are colleagues.
They share our desire to create a society that
recognises that all persons have a right to live
and work freely. They have joined this struggle
to make it visible through their work.

Have you been part of any art project before?
No, this is the first time.

Do you think this project has influenced
you in any way?
I discovered how art can be used to make
our struggle visible. I discovered how
a participative dynamic can be used to
channel mutual support and solidarity, in
order to denounce and change our situation.

Bliss Park is an artwork, a skatepark and a new civic space for the borough of St Helens. It is commissioned and produced by local young people and skateboarders, together with artists Heather Peak and Ivan Morison from the creative practice, Studio Morison.

This conversation took place in St Helens between Allan Davidge, owner of 51st Skate, Sam Lee, a local skateboarder and Suzanne Dempsey Sawin, a producer from Heart of Glass.

Suzanne Dempsey Sawin **Please briefly describe what this project is and why you've taken part in it.**

Sam Lee This project is about developing a new space for skaters to hang out and enjoy. I got involved through the skate shop. As soon as Allan got approached he put it to us and asked us for our input. I was like "well, if this park's going to happen then we can't just sit back and expect the artist to design it, we've got to give our input."

SDS It's a full circle isn't it? We wouldn't be able to do it without you and you would end up with something completely useless to you. What is Studio Morison to you?

SL The creative side of the design of the park.

Allan Davidge I don't think it would be where it is now without everybody that has come together. It really has just made it bigger than I expected it ever would be. Even now it surprises me how far it's gone – the concept design of the park is beyond what I'd ever had imagined. If it had been left to us we'd have basically built the same as any other generic skate park. But then Stephen King, who is a skater and artist consulting on the project,

www.cappnetwork.com/capp-project/
st-helens-skatepark-project/

came across and made us look at all these spots all over the world that became famous, but are not actually skate parks. He challenged us to try and incorporate these things into a park, and obviously Heather and Ivan have taken on all of what we've said into one design. The skaters have looked at it and thought "oh, we could skate it this way, that way".

SL Skaters see things differently. You look at a banked wall and see just part of the building. But a skater looks at it as an element for doing things with.

AD Our conversations opened eyes to what art is from a skater's point of view: something that can be skated. And I think this has opened Ivan's eyes. When artists have done pieces for public places, people will look at them and be like "oh, yeah", whereas skaters appreciate it because they take into every little aspect of how it's shaped and how it can be skated.

SDS Do you consider yourselves to be artists as skaters?

SL I wouldn't say I'm an artist, but I would say that skateboarding is an art form.

AD I'd say skateboarding is an art because of how much you put into it. You are expressing yourself.

SDS Do you think this project would have worked in a different way if it had not been proposed by an artist?

SL It wouldn't have had that extra bit of life to it.

AD They were brilliant in what they've brought to the project; Ivan's expressed himself into the park and that's something that people are going to appreciate. It isn't just a skate park, it's something a lot bigger.

SL A lot of people will come from all over the country just to skate this park. It's going to challenge people. There will parts of it that even the developers will look at and go "no one will skate that high". But then, skaters will find a way!

AD Yeah, skaters see things differently.

We Will See! acquainted blind people with visual artists, their working methods and their visual language. Meanwhile, the blind people who took part introduced the artists to their own way of way of 'seeing'.

Márta Jáger was one of five visually impaired persons who took part in the project. She worked together with artist Kamilla Szíj.

This conversation took place in Budapest between Márta Jáger and Andrea Simon, Head of International Relations at Ludwig Múzeum Budapest.

Briefly describe the project in which you took part.
The title of our project, *We Will See!*, reflects on the notion that we did not know from the beginning what would grow out of our collaboration, but we were certain it would be something valuable.

I selected Kamilla based on her voice and her first few sentences. I sensed that she is aim-oriented, strong-minded but modest. I believe that we both were fascinated and impressed by the other. During our project I drew a picture that was important for me in the air and Kamilla followed me in synchrony. Between us there was a piece of glass, so Kamilla drew on the glass. Kamilla's drawing was later engraved into the glass, so it became physically tangible and long lasting. The work process was filmed and a small documentary film was made.

Why did you join the project?
I heard about the project from a special education teacher. When I was a child, I used to draw a lot and nowadays my favourite activity is weaving. It appealed to me to be part of something special with an artist being on my side.

www.cappnetwork.com/capp-project/
we-will-see/

Briefly describe your role within the project.
My biggest challenge was to become open enough towards Kamilla so that we could find a common voice. When we had our plan, I had to figure out what I would like to draw in the air. We completed the drawing in a morning. I recommended that I draw the picture several times. This proved to be a good idea as it then looks more complex for the viewer. After that I formulated my sentences for the film and recorded them.

What is an artist to you?
I think everyone is an artist who holds themselves as such.

What was Kamilla Szíj to you?
The process and result of our joint work is shared by both of us. Kamilla's style, thinking and character are very close to mine: precise, meticulous, persistent and demanding. I was lucky to have chosen her.

Do you have taken part in any other art project before?
An exhibition called *Living Folk Art* in the Hungarian Museum of Ethnography in 2015 included a few of my art pieces, and I was awarded the 3rd prize.

Do you consider that this project has had some kind of influence on you? If yes, what?
I was enthusiastic and curious to start the project. After becoming acquainted with Kamilla and her works, it was important to create something that we both could value. All of our conversations were like a delightful adventure. It was useful to think through, rethink and formulate the process of me drawing in my head. Since then, I use it more consciously, and the movements have became faster and more precise. The most important thing is to make my objects beautiful. With Kamilla, I understood and felt deep inside what being an artist and creating an artwork really means. The point is that the creator expresses something from within him or herself.

Would this project have worked in a different way if it would not have been proposed by an artist?
Once I wrote a harsher than necessary letter to Kamilla, I regretted this very much. Kamilla was also inclined to pronounce her thoughts immediately, we were very similar in that sense as well. Fortunately, no one was offended. During the creation process, we were able to work together very well, we used the available time to the maximum. I do not think that I would do anything differently.

Traveller Collection is a project by the Irish artist Seamus Nolan that investigates the idea of archive, deconstructs ideas of 'heritage', engages with communities of place and of interest, and involves Traveller activists and archivists.

This conversation took place in Dublin, Ireland between Martin Collins, Co-director of Pavee Point Traveller and Roma Centre, and Seamus Nolan.

Briefly describe the project in which you took part.
It looks at the idea of a 'Traveller Museum' – what would it mean to the Traveller community, how would it work and what would be in it?

Why did you become involved in the project?
We became involved as the celebration and promotion of Traveller Culture and Heritage is one of the strategic aims of Pavee Point. Traveller culture and identity have been denigrated and ignored for too long in Irish society. Promotion and celebration of Traveller culture is now one of the actions in the Government's National Traveller and Roma Inclusion Strategy – NTRIS.

Briefly describe your role within the project.
Our role was to facilitate communication with the Traveller community, and also we house a substantial collection of material that might feature in a Traveller Museum – along with the Dept of Folkore UCD and the Irish Film Institute.

www.cappnetwork.com/capp-project/
traveller-collection/

What is an artist to you?
An artist is different things to different people. In terms of community, an artist is someone who produces a reflection that allows that community to better understand itself.

What am I to you?
You are becoming a familiar face to more and more people working here, and you are calm and focused presence in what can sometimes be a high energy setting.

Have you taken part in any other art project before?
Pavee Point has always had cultural activity at its core. We established the Traveller Cultural and Heritage Centre in 1990 and have been involved in numerous projects with Travellers and non-Travellers in visual arts, music, drama, storytelling, photography, video and craft.

Do you consider that this project is having or has had some kind of influence on you?
It's giving a stronger focus to the idea of a Traveller archive or museum. As our organisation does not have core funding for this work it is sometimes difficult to give these things the time they deserve. We hope it will be a valuable resource for Travellers in the future.

Do you think this project would work in a different way if it had not been proposed by an artist?
It is useful for the project to be led by someone who comes from the world of art and culture, who is familiar with its structures, language, codes etc. This is a world that is often outside the experience of marginalised groups.

Participation

The dialogue on participation took form of a conversation via email with two CAPP artists, Sibylle Peters and Ernesto Pujol, as well as with Cornelia Stertz, who took part in the workshops and the group performance *Systems of Weight* led by Ernesto Pujol as artist-in-residence at Kunsthalle Osnabrück in 2016. The conversation looked at participatory practice from different points of view in order to question key issues such as: motivations of the artist and non-artist to open up to collaboration, decision making, challenges of communication, hierarchical structures and the definition of roles. The questions were posed by Julia Draganovic, Director of Kunsthalle Osnabrück.

Julia Draganovic The first challenge one has to face when conceiving a participatory project is how to convince people to participate. Cornelia, why did you participate in Ernesto's project?

Cornelia Stertz I came because I knew about Ernesto. His medium is the body, his strategy is silence and his method is listening.

JD Sibylle, with *Playing Up* and *Kaputt – The Academy of Destruction*, you adopted existing formats like the game and the academy; you sort of hijacked those formats in order to turn the hierarchies contained within them upside down. Is reaching out to have people participate a challenge for you?

Sibylle Peters Of course, *Playing Up* and *Kaputt* adopt existing formats and somehow hijack them. This might help with participation, as participants can partly rely on given knowledge instead of being alienated: most people know what it means to play a game and to follow an instruction, and many people know what it means to take part in an learning environment or academy of some kind. And if they don't, for example because they are too young, it is lovely to have them have their first experience of an academy with *Kaputt*. However, the hijacking of formats is not the main tool when it comes to reaching out and inviting people to participate in a project in the first place. The general invitation to participate is about the impetus of things one strongly longs for instead: almost all projects by Theatre of Research are based on strong and very popular desires. With *Kaputt*, this is quite simply the strong desire for destruction that many children and adults have in common. How strong this desire really is became clear to us during the public play-ins we did with *Playing Up*. Here, the cards which included some form of destruction proved to be the most popular. To me, participatory projects have to be popular in this sense – participation is not a value in itself, it has to be triggered by the chance to do something participants really want to do.

JD Ernesto, you call yourself a "social choreographer". How does that term describe your participatory practice?

Ernesto Pujol: I call myself a social choreographer because I do not choreograph a company of dancers. I choreograph regular citizens. I seek to work with a mixture of trained and untrained bodies, so as to manifest the true physical range of the people in a village, town or city.

I believe that we construct the society that we wish to live in. And I believe in a participatory society. Therefore, my projects start with a conversational process through which I have a dialogue with as many citizens as possible, with gatekeepers and stakeholders, listening to their memories, knowledge, opinions and reactions. I identify project advisors and partners. I create a structure that supervises me; I create my own accountability. Then, I begin to elaborate a proposal. I sustain a transparent process in which I share my evolving ideas, back and forth.

Once my proposal has been thus approved, project recruitment begins with an open call. I begin to work, balancing trained and untrained bodies, absorbing and processing a wide range of advice and feedback about evolving gestures.

JD Ernesto, I am interested in questions of decision-making. It was fascinating to observe how you create awareness about decisions that have to be taken by each person in the group. But where is the limit, what do you claim as your responsibility and where does the freedom of others begin?

EP The freedom of working with me is not apparent at first. It is like the freedom found within monastic experience. At first, a monastery can look like a prison. But little by little, it begins to open up psychically. People begin to realise that, within the minimal menu of gestures I have proposed to them, there is

an infinite number of variations if they take the time to trust, to explore, to remember, to think, and to feel more and more. I am always ready to step in and correct something. I want them to take risks within the boundaries that we have agreed to. I am going to take risks with them, even the risk of choreographic violations if they are necessary for a particular performer and create an unexpected but refreshing or memorable counterpoint. It is a very complex equation, partly based on past experiences, knowledge of the human condition and empathy. Ultimately, all of the freedom I give is based on empathy.

JD Cornelia, if you think back to working with Ernesto, what does this experience mean to you now, after almost two years?

CS I am still fond of thinking back to this. The group of silent walkers became a community, which greeted everybody that entered or exited the nave of the former church with deep respect and empathy. This was very impressive for me to witness. I feel a deep gratitude for those who accompanied me.

JD Ernesto, how do you manage to gain trust in the people you work with?

EP I believe that the only way to conduct a socially engaged art practice is through an unconditional act of trust in people. Perhaps this belief comes from the fact that I was the son of immigrant parents. I have experienced the challenge of being distrusted by a society as a foreign element. I know the hard labor of having to earn the trust of a people.

I do not want anyone to have to undergo that terrible process for me or for my project. Therefore, people do not have to earn my trust. I have learned that trust generates trust.

Of course, I have witnessed violent political processes and experienced discriminatory social moments. Trust can be betrayed. There were moments in projects when I have had to withdraw my trust from someone because they were hurting the group. But I chose to believe in the potential of humanity, making projects where trust gives it the time and space to expand.

JD Sibylle, the trust that you as the artist show towards the people with whom you play and work and learn is extraordinary. You not only put children in responsible roles, but you also give them tools that most parents are afraid to hand out to them. What is the secret behind this confidence? And, have there ever been moments where you had to intervene in an authoritarian way to protect someone?

SP Of course, I have to intervene sometimes. I'm not sure if that is authoritarian though.

Just last week we had a performance with a big group of children who had a habit of being pretty nasty towards each other. Right before the performance started, charged up with adrenalin, some of the children got into a fight. I witnessed a big boy pressing a cushion onto the face of a much smaller girl. I screamed "Stop!" and to be honest, I think I actually said "Stop! Fucking hell, what's going on here?" And somehow it worked, as everybody immediately stopped and looked at me: I had said a bad, forbidden word. I had lost it. I didn't hide that what I saw pushed me out of the controlled frame of support and facilitation. I didn't use my authority so much as making it clear with my reaction that what happened was far beyond the line of acceptable behaviour.

This, of course, does not explain what might be 'the secret' of confidence in participants, and particularly in children. In my experience, people, and maybe especially children, will adapt fast to the way they are addressed. If their words and contributions are taken seriously and seen as important, the contributions will quickly become serious and important. I'm a strong opponent of concepts of development, which seem to know and therefore prescribe what children at a certain age will understand and will be able to contribute. I do not understand at all why adults, in their communication with children, carefully try to avoid everything children might not understand. I think this approach is highly counterproductive for everyone. All of us are constantly confronted with parts of the world we don't understand. Children are used to this even more than adults, and they have many strategies to deal with what they don't understand. While, of course, at the Theatre of Research we try to make everything accessible, i.e. find a way in for everybody, this doesn't mean avoiding everything that might not immediately be understandable for all.

JD How important is language for your projects?

SP Coming out of a world completely governed by books, Theatre of Research seemed to me to be all about material, movement, feelings, games and experiments. However I have to admit that Theatre of Research is still very much language based. I don't think that I'm the right person to overcome that. Actually, having a PhD in German Literature, I'm not convinced that it makes sense to call something research which is not using language, at least when it comes to pose questions and to share results. I only worked once with kids with whom I didn't share a language. I didn't do it again, as I spent the whole project envying the translator. She, it appeared to me, had all the fun, while I felt cut off from the all the important dialogue with the participating kids.

JD Ernesto, as you were working in a country whose language you do not speak, do you think that not understanding can be fertile?

EP I believe that we communicate in verbal and nonverbal ways. We also communicate through emotion, expressed in tone and volume, and through mannerisms, through the body. When someone speaks, I pay attention to the fullness of their communication. Nevertheless, there is no question that to work in a country whose official language I do not speak is a challenge. I depend on translators, and I depend on my instinct and intuition. But mostly, I depend on my vulnerability, on my willingness to become vulnerable, and on their willingness to become vulnerable with me. It is embarrassing, but it forces a certain kind of openness, a willingness to transcend barriers.

CS Between me and Ernesto, language was not important at all. There was no real language barrier, although we do not speak a common language. Ernesto had trust in me and although I do not understand English, through Ernesto's actions I did not feel excluded but part of it all.

JD Last but not least, Ernesto and Sibylle: how would you define the role of the people involved in your projects?

EJ Over time, I have moved away from calling myself an artist and I have begun to understand myself more broadly as a maker of culture. Art is only one of the many elements that compose culture.

Therefore, I approach my collaborators as human beings. They are creative human beings who seek outlets to explore and manifest their creativity. I engaged these "creatives" as accomplices in the making of a meaningful aesthetic experience that explores something about the memory of a people, the history of a place. I risked going deep and sharing it publicly, perhaps to release it, discuss it and begin to heal it. We make culture together. And because we make it together, they co-own it.

SP I think that all really great participatory projects find new ways of participation and collaboration, which fit with the character of the project itself. To invent participatory and collaborative protocols is a big part of inventing the project as such. Therefore, there is no good general answer to this question. While everybody who takes an active part in any part of a project is a participant, those children/people I work with more intensely would usually be called co-researchers. But in reality nobody is ever really called participant or co-researcher, instead a good project will provide better, more specific names or titles for the different parts people play.

Ernesto Pujol is a performance artist and social choreographer. He is the author of Walking Art Practice, Reflections on Socially Engaged Paths, *Triarchy Press. Pujol has roots in Spain, Cuba and Puerto Rico. He is based in New York.*

Professor Sibylle Peters is head of the PhD programme Performing Citizenship in Hamburg, Guest Professor for Transdisciplinary Design at the Folkwang University Essen, and co-founder and Director of Theatre of Research. As a performance artist, she focuses on participation and collective research (often with Geheimagentur performance collective).

Cornelia Stertz has one daughter and works as an employee. Practicing yoga as a leisure time activity, she understood that this is her vocation and started to practice meditation. She changed her thinking, developed empathy and is more connected to other people now.

Julia Draganovic (PhD) is Director of Kunsthalle Osnabrück, founding member of LaRete Art Projects, board member of No Longer Empty, New York and President of IKT International Association of Curators of Contemporary Art. She is interested in the role art can play for social improvement.

Process

For the dialogue on process, Minna Tarka and Jussi Koitela from m-cult, invited CAPP artists Dafna Maimon and Valentina Karga, and Tate Liverpool's Head of Learning Lindsey Fryer, to discuss contemporary artistic collaborative processes. Of the dialogue, Minna and Jussi comment: We wanted to understand how these processes are negotiated and orchestrated within the conditions of artistic practice and institutional structures.

We wanted to focus on how process-based work is always localised, and born within a certain context. For m-cult, these questions relate to the experience of commissioning collaborative projects in the Helsinki Maunula neighbourhood within CAPP. How could these process-based works be uprooted from their social and material context, and shared, presented or exhibited elsewhere?

For the artist, an 'end result' or 'outcome' has to be framed to fit the project management culture of institutions and funders. The artists also face the demand to accumulate artistic merit via solo exhibitions and performances hosted by institutions. Further questions include how process-based work is compensated, for both artists and participants.

How can institutions change in order to host this type of work? For example, Tate Liverpool has developed new ways to facilitate and present collaborative processes during the CAPP project. Finally, we wanted to address the role of documentation as a means of sharing and extending processes. Can documentation provide us with 'stand alone' formats reaching beyond the here and now of the artistic process?

We devised this dialogue as a combination of three Skype discussions. During the discussions we encouraged participants to also think about ideal conditions for process-based practice.

Minna Tarkka and Jussi Koitela: How do you consider duration and time in your artistic process, and in relation to project management and institutional structures?

Dafna Maimon Processes are what I do – I have stopped using the word 'project' because it determines an end result, as if you would start working just to execute whatever that project is. I work in a way where things often mutate over several forms and each time I recontextualise it into the space. Of course, that is what people generally do – change the installation to suit different spaces. But in my case it's even more than that; I start with a stream-of-consciousness from which things come out over an extended period of time, and then let these side narratives come out.

Sometimes this results in a difficult situation: what is the work, this one or that one, this title or that title? I don't want to define things that way, but I keep showing some form of results that are like the end of a chapter. A lot of people are not comfortable with showing things in the making, but my work is so process-based and the performances are improvised – not improvised as they are shown, but the results of multiple improvisations. I will never write a script and ask someone to say exactly what I wrote. So it is quite natural to let people into the process.

Let's say you're dealing with space for a performance. In order to facilitate the performance you need rehearsal time, you need the time to do the installation, but also the time to develop the performance. Exhibition schedules usually have a slot of one or maybe three months for a project. This is problematic, because you are often asked to do a lot of things at the same time – an opening, a performance, an artist's talk – which affects the possible quality of what the performance could be.

On the one hand, you have to create a thing that is really good, but you also have to make sure that your life doesn't become such that you feel depleted after spending months of work on something that is only on for one evening. How would I be able to facilitate a thing, to put all this love and work into a process, so that it doesn't just end with a 40-minute performance? Sometimes I take it in my own hands and try to create a different structure. So this is also a demand for the institutions – are you willing to support things that are not just opening spectacles?

Valentina Karga At some point it became important for me to disassociate my process from the commission process. It is not really possible to get something back in a terms of money or publicity value from everything I do, because I just do too much. At first, I saw this as something negative, but then I realised that it is normal because I do this 24 hours a day, even when I sleep. Understanding this gave me a lot of time and space to breathe; I could be even more productive, not caring if the things I do will appear somewhere because I want to do them anyway. Instead of monetary compensation, you will build friendships or get more information to fill some gaps of your research. You can simply spend your time more meaningfully. The most important thing for me is to be always sincere to yourself and to your interests. If you do something to sell or because it is wanted from you, then you feel pressured.

JK In your collaborations, have you experienced struggles or differences in understanding the value of artistic work?

VK Sometimes with exhibitions you need to discuss how work is valued. Like now with the totem project I am doing for the Thailand Biennale, a continuation of the collaboration I did with m-cult. The best way was obviously to stay there for some months to produce it, but the institution does not offer this. I told them, it is not possible to do it otherwise. I can't build it somewhere else and just ship it to you, because it has to be made with the local people. So we entered into a dialogue and I

argued that I don't need time just to develop a concept but also to develop the production. In the end we agreed that the compensation will not be an artist fee but a labour fee.

JK What about compensation for participants; have you thought of that, Dafna?

DM There's a lot of computing between alternatives: either you pay someone to execute something, or create situations where people can participate of their own free will. In the *I am Hungry* process with Related Primates I have to say I felt slightly hindered as an artist. Maybe that's my own problem, but I felt the pressure to continuously give something to the participants because they were not paid.

MT Lindsey, listening to the artists it becomes clear that the art institutions have to change in order to enable process-based work. It seems that Tate Liverpool is trying to do that, to manifest a new type of space at the gallery?

Lindsey Fryer Yes we're trying. The Tate Liverpool vision is to become much more emotionally connected with audiences from an institutional point of view, rather than a technical relationship of a publicly funded organisation with free entry to collections. But if the public doesn't feel that it is for them, then we have a problem. Quite often when we're commissioning artists to work with people, the work is off-site and doesn't have a serious manifestation within the institution.

Within the CAPP project, we took the opportunity to really think about making this kind of socially engaged, collaborative practice more visible by inhabiting the space of the institution. Normally our top floor gallery has three shows a year for the paying public. One of those shows was taken out of the programme and we were left with an annual slot that we were able to colonise with collaborative projects. Initially, and perhaps inevitably, this was seen by the institution as a learning project rather than as an artist commission or artist residency. So we had a lot of internal misconceptions going on; it is very difficult to change the culture of thinking quickly. As an institution we naturally are part of a learning process: thinking, shifting, changing, examining – and we need to make sure that we have curators who want to take the journey with us.

In *O.K. - The Musical*, the artist Christopher Kline was so well organised. We had confidence to develop the relationship with our communities on the back of that really well structured process. We inhabited the gallery space, which was open to the public while the process was going on. We even had

an information assistant in the gallery, and people just walked in and built a relationship with the artist, and then came back and sometimes took part. So I suppose even if the performance is part of the work, I don't see the difference between the process itself and the end of the process when it was again open to the public as performances. But everything before that was visible – and I think that the key is making the invisible visible in a way that is sensitive to the artist's work and the constituencies, to the public that they're working with, and to the needs of the institution itself.

It was hard work. As a curator you were present all day, every day for a month. And it doesn't stop: we're still working with the artist now, a year on. In terms of resources, it challenged the institution's use of spaces, and ways of working with the art handling team, electricians, everyone.

MT What about practices of documentation? Valentina and Dafna, many of your works are performative or realised in public space, is there a way to present those in a white cube gallery via documents or otherwise? Have you developed strategies of documentation that would work in and out of the process context?

VK The public works are not really for the white cube; I'm not interested in bringing works into a context where they were not made. But I would think of a translation of earlier work based on a new context that might be a white cube. Taking account of how many people visit this space, what sort of people, who is running the place, where it is located and what the neighbourhood is like. I think you should approach documentation so that you are making a new work, even if the work is based on earlier work. And straightforward documentation is different from using documentation material to create a new piece.

DM The actual happening is the work, but the photos and video that are created around it and the material objects are a part of the tangible working process. They can be used as artefacts to show in a gallery installation, but also to work things further. In the Conglomerate collective, we are five artists trying to understand the problem of documentation. While making big installations or large performance projects, how should we deal with the fact that we put so much energy into the work, which ends up as some pictures online? We arrived at a model where the installation functions as a set, and we specifically write scripts that become a film – a work on its own.

LF At Tate we do a lot more filming. We have recorded personal testimonies and produced a 'making of' film, but it is difficult to show these outside the context. The documentation could be more about telling the story in an emotional way, perhaps in the future it could become even a feature film?

JK and MT So what would you consider ideal conditions for working with and on process?

VK Maybe you don't have to think about these so exclusively because you just work and then things happen. We don't need to be so fixed, to always understand or control the process. I am just part of the process, I am not the process itself. It has been a relief to finally understand that I don't need to control and predict everything: the process knows better than me. The process has agency.

LF If it was up to me, we would be working like this all the time, interweaving other ways, concepts, practices within the programme and organisational structure. It really needs to be a space where people feel welcome, own the space, inhabit the space. The gallery should be like a library, a visual conceptual resource for cultural production.

Valentina Karga is an artist and architect based in Berlin. Her collaborative piece Our Coming Community *was part of m-cult's CAPP residency in Helsinki 2016.*

Dafna Maimon is a performance and video artist and part of the Related Primates ensemble. She produced the collaborative process I am Hungry *commissioned by Agora Collective and KW Institute for Contemporary Art in 2017.*

Lindsey Fryer is Head of Learning at Tate Liverpool. During the CAPP programme, she led the commissions Art Gym *by Assemble and Tate Collective in 2016, and* O.K. - The Musical *by Christopher Kline in 2017.*

Minna Tarkka is a producer, researcher, educator, and curator of media art and participatory culture. As Director of m-cult, she has been responsible for the overall management of the CAPP project activities in Helsinki.

Jussi Koitela is a freelance curator. He has acted as a curatorial advisor for m-cult's collaborative arts commissions for CAPP.

Politics

The dialogue on the politics of collaborative arts practice took place in London on 21 February 2018. Convened by Lois Keidan of the Live Art Development Agency (LADA), the discussion involved Barby Asante from the UK, Seamus Nolan from Ireland and, via Skype, Fotini Lazaridou-Hatzigoga from Greece. Each artist had been commissioned to deliver projects as part of CAPP. Later, Bence Zsin from Hungary, an artist commissioned by Ludwig Múzeum, offered his written interruptions to the discussion.

Lois Keidan: I hope we'll be able to take two different approaches to our brief today, about the politics of working together as artists, and about the power relations involved in working with participants to a socially-engaged agenda. It's about ownership, authorship and ethics, but also about the political potential of these practices, and where the power and agency lies in the relationship with the institutions that often fund and host this work.

Barby Asante Speaking from my own position, and in relation to works with people from so-called 'marginalised' backgrounds, I've made a choice to work with people, but not to use it as a way of addressing or fixing problems. I create and instigate the situations; most of my work is giving agency to young people so they can be actors in culture. One of the things I've done is create a collective in which black, brown and queer young people can talk about growing up in this country. What has disturbed me is the way some institutions pick out participants as 'excluded', but they never seem to progress into any other position. My choice to create that collective was an action against the institutional violence that is so often enacted against these participants.

LK So you removed yourself from the institution?

BA It's not that we don't ever work in institutions, but we make sure that we give agency to those groups who are considered 'underrepresented'. Often that work is co-opted by institutions; Teresa Cisneros (who I was originally working with) and I ended up switching our focus and instead trying to work on changing the structure of the institution through working with its core staff. So thinking about socially-engaged practice as something that's not necessarily out there, but actually *inside*.

Seamus Nolan I completely get what you're saying. I always consider that I work for the organisation that I've been commissioned by, and interrogate what that organisation is trying to do. It's the *context* of the participation that I'm interested in. I'm interested in where the space for my voice is, and if there's a space for my voice, then there's a space for other voices, too. If I was to describe my practice, sometimes I would say it was more socially *dis*-engaged than socially engaged. I find there is a dominant model of how art practice is effective and I think it's premised on a failure. It's always based on the fact that society is failing. To be socially engaged in that process, I think is to be complicit in that failure. To interrupt that failure is where there is a chance to create some kind of change.

LK Do you feel like you have a responsibility to affect change within the institution as well, as Barby does?

SN I think the institution has to adapt to the work that is created. I understand the contradiction of it; if it's a failure, you interrupt the failure to make it fail better.

Fotini Lazaridou-Hatzigoga I come from architecture so I'm very interested in structures and how forms of organisation allow things to happen or prevent other things from happening. An important thing has always been to push away from the idea of an audience, and move more towards an idea of a public. I appreciate what Barby was saying about starting projects which give agency to others; being clear about what you're bringing and offering. It's a never-ending learning process, especially when finding ways to make people heard.

Bence Zsin Most collaborative arts projects do not pay enough attention to the fact that commitment is a long-term process and part of collective learning. A project can only be authentic and honest if there is trust within the group, and between the group and artists. When working with groups from disadvantaged backgrounds, I concentrate on them. It is an inspiring route, and allows us to focus on a joyful process of creation together.

LK There's been a real institutional embrace of socially engaged practices here in the UK, but many opportunities are focused on asking artists to go into housing estates and make people feel better about their shit conditions, rather than money being spent on improving those conditions. It does feel like the ethos of some of these socially engaged practices has been appropriated by institutions.

BA I totally agree but I think it's more than that. It's a colonial history that has formed many of these institutions, and they're rarely willing to face the colonial perspective they operate from. They say "we want to invite you in, but on our terms". The problematics of these projects are repeated over and over again.

BZ Institutions can have very diverse roles in the lives of communities, though. My experiences in South Hungary prove that the institution's involvement is essential to foster large-scale projects with long-term effects. Not long ago I worked with people suffering from addictions and in this situation it was the institution, apart from financial security, which provided the feeling of security, trust and community.

LK Which projects transcend some of the more troubling systems, and create agency in new ways?

SN The Rom Archive sounds pretty amazing. It really is collaborative, in terms of the grassroots community, the organisers, the curators, and then the government departments that are funding it. It's curators and organisations from a Roma and Sinti background, working together with artists and collectors. When certain decisions need to be made, the organisers will even step away from the table so they don't influence what it becomes.

LK It's really important we can point to things that work, or should I say things that fail better, in order to demonstrate different ways of working.

BA I had been thinking about these issues following the 2011 London – really thinking about the presence, the real physical thing, of young people of colour. I decided then that I wasn't going to do it in the way that an institution wants me to do it, so in 2014 Teresa and I brought together a collective called Sorryyoufeeluncomfortable. Supporting them brought us out of an institutional framework and into a care framework, but that meant we had to respond to their wish to be seen, and to make actions, and be willing to facilitate that with our address books and our reputations. This is something that I didn't have when I was 24, but why not? Why shouldn't I have been contributing to culture in a certain way? My daughter said to me the other day "wow, I'm third generation", but she is still seen as having just arrived. We need to move on from a state of arrival to a place where we are making our impact, in culture and from a political position. It's about creating the conditions where people can be seen and flourish. It's not going to be me that's the legacy of that; I don't want people to create in exactly my image. It's the failure of institutions that they want people to do things exactly as they would do them.

BZ When I am working with people from disadvantaged backgrounds, I always think about the possibility that the participants would rather spend the project budget differently. It is crucial to remind myself that I am not there to change their circumstances, but as a visual artist who can offer some kind of experience that we can enjoy together. The problems will not disappear, but something happens between us, including me as part of the group, that is important. So I do not look at this group members as people with problems, rather as people who know something about life that I do not know. And I can understand their knowledge though getting to know them.

FL-H There are a few institutions which have been experimenting with the idea of titles and credits, how the work is organised within a given group, and how everyone can be put up on the same level. It comes back to this question of openness which has been bugging me over the years. There are lots of places which proclaim themselves as being open, but in reality there are a number of invisible borders. Language is a part of this, and the defining of roles.

LK That's a beautiful segue into the political potential of these practices at cultural, societal, policy and grassroots levels. One of the challenges is around hierarchies of form, and how different models and art forms fit into an institution's understanding of what art can be, who it can be for, and what it can do.

SN The professionalisation of the terminology assumes there's some kind of competency in the first place. I became an artist because I didn't like school, and I discovered there was a gap where I could just produce something and it be about whatever I wanted. The Traveller community I'm working with at the moment has such a low rate of second-level schooling, and third-level is almost zero, but the history of engagement and socially engaged practice makes me into a professional who is educating, which I find really problematic.

I don't really have anything to teach; I can just spot the pitfalls maybe, or try to guide things a little bit, but it's not a profession, it's an instinct. The institution requires that complex professionalism in order to be at that larger table, and the artist requires it in order to be at the institutional table, but then we're all just bringing the same rhetoric.

BA I'm going to talk from a slightly different position, because there is a problem in the way that artists had to become professional, but then many students and young people are being told "no, you can't make it in that way". That's part of the reason half these kids are not at school, because they are being told that their culture is not valid. We talk about having a seat at the table, something which is said in particular by a number of black women right now, but there is a skilling up that is really important in order to arrive at validation, and that's what I can bring as an artist. I'm interested in having a professionalism, and using it to find a way for other people to also come to the table. Once they're at that table, maybe they'll want to be at the table at a policy meeting, where it's not actually *done to them*, but that they have a stake in.

LK The artist and activist John Jordan famously said that art gets in the way of social change because it's reduced to art. People can hide behind it.

FL-H I was thinking about how important it is that projects find ways to relate the forms of the project to the forms of the institution, and what kind of conflicts and discrepancies might arise between the two. By doing that, we can try to challenge the politics of the institution themselves, which might be quite difficult. Asking small questions about working conditions, contracts, how the press release is written, who gets invited to what kind of event... There might be a way to reorganise some of these relationships through collaborative or socially engaged practices, and create some small trembles which could have a bigger effect.

SN I really think it's important that people are tooled-up, but I worry that unless you have those tools, you are completely powerless. That reinforces the idea that operating outside an institutional framework means you are powerless and invisible. I hope art finds ways for the invisible to become visible, and not just through the institutions.

Barby Asante is an artist, curator, educator and occasional DJ. Her work is concerned with the politics of place, space, identity, and the histories and legacies of colonialism. Asante realised a CAPP commission in 2018, convening women of colour to enact a performative Declaration of Independence.

Fotini Lazaridou-Hatzigoga works between art, architecture and urban research to explore the possibilities in the intersections between social and physical spaces. In 2015, Lazaridou-Hatzigoga delivered a CAPP workshop which took the form of a publishing experiment for the communities of a small street in Berlin-Neukölln.

Seamus Nolan is an artist whose practice investigates the relative value of objects and social processes as they appear within different economies and contexts. Nolan worked with Irish Traveller communities on a large CAPP commission during 2017-18.

Bence Zsin is an artist from Budapest, creating paintings, performances and installations. He lives and works in Pécs, where he is a DLA student at the University of Pécs. Zsin was commissioned to create Floating Home *by the Ludwig Múzeum for CAPP.*

Lois Keidan is Co-Director of the Live Art Development Agency, a CAPP partner organisation based in London, UK.

Place

The dialogue on place took the form of three interviews with CAPP artists, Selina Thompson, Mark Storor and Francisco Rubio. Commenting on the interviews Chrissie Tiller writes:

'I never quite managed to get Selina Thompson, Mark Storor and Francisco Rubio in the same place. Instead, each conversation I had fed into the next. Rubio speaks of the skein that links their work with different communities. I would like people to read this piece as such a skein: a length of thread, loosely knotted together.

I want to thank each of my interviewees for the generosity with which they shared their responses, and the wealth of experience and understanding of this work they brought to the dialogue. And to Heart of Glass and CAPP for asking me to open these conversations.'

Francisco Rubio (LaFundició)

On CAPP
We became engaged with CAPP when were invited by hablarenarte to write a brief text on failure. Failure seems to involve some sort of moral evaluation, but in trying to escape this dichotomy between success and failure we understood what we do is to place ourselves within a situation, taking part in it as just one more agent with our own specific awareness and sensitivity towards the context.

On place
The physical place is important, but for us it is more about social, political and cultural relations in the sense of a situated practice. Contemporary art frequently tries to hide the social and political relations with which the artwork is intertwined. The supposedly neutral white cube hides the inequalities that support the structures of the art world and the artwork itself.

Our own space is located on the outskirts of Barcelona. It is a place belonging to the city council where they allocate homes to people who have been in receipt of social programmes. People are caught up in their own situations and social services approach them as individual cases, but our main intention is to become a community that shares these problems and faces them in a collective way. Place is important because all this is happening in a specific place and we need to consider how we take care of it, how we see it and live it.

On collaborators
We need to work with a wide network of people. We are in close contact with social movements in the city. But we also try to establish close relationships with our immediate neighbours, creating a skein of connections that runs from the block to the neighbourhood to the metropolitan area.

The range of each collaboration is different. Someone can be directly involved in a project whereas others participate in a more tangential way. For example, for two years we have been working in a process called the *Interpretation Centre of the City from the Shanty Towns*. It's about rescuing the memory of these former shanty towns – in some ways a completely forgotten history. The people who first came here were mainly immigrants from rural areas of Spain. We think we can learn something today from the way they organised human space and how they sorted the city. So, two years ago we started to work with a smallish group who has been engaged with us researching and gathering pictures to make an archive of the shanty town. This group then

started to propose actions and share some of the research, and engage more people in the project. We involved the wider population by encouraging them to understand how the city has evolved historically from the '70s to now.

On safe spaces
It's difficult for me to imagine art/culture as a 'safe space' – it makes me think of an isolated space. On the contrary, I think we have to expose the social, political and environmental context within this space.

We worry that collaborative art practice can sometimes be used as a tool for pacification. Conflict in terms of struggle against oppression is not bad in itself. Collaborative art should be a tool for social struggle not social cohesion. Part of our fear is the inclusion of collaborative art in the institutional art world – just like any another art discipline. We're concerned this will lead to a neutralisation of a practice that should be completely intertwined with its social milieu.

On time
When we started to work as a co-operative in 2006, we were going around proposing projects in different contexts and communities. In 2013, we realised we never had time to deepen or set up strong links with the different actors involved in those

contexts. So, we decided to be established in one place. Since then we try to work with a more eco-systemic perspective. Our practice develops on a daily basis and evolves in time as we work with different agents, initiatives and tools – just like ordinary life, with no idea of an ending.

On international meetings
We have to have in mind the global flows and situations that condition even our relationships with our closest neighbours. In that sense any social and political project must have a global approach. In the field of collaborative art, we could also say there has been a predominance of Anglo-Saxon discourse. It's important that people from other parts of the world can also contribute to this discourse from their own particular situations and context to enrich the debate.

Selina Thompson

On place
It's interesting to think about place as opposed to situation. As a black artist and part of the African diaspora, I feel it's always political and social: we are all settlers or displaced. The history of place is too violent for it to be anything other.

In the CAPP project, I was initially trying to get a sense of how rural Irish whiteness defines itself where there isn't necessarily a racialised other. The areas I was working in are places where the immigration of black people is still perceived as relatively new; first and second generations. Which is always a particularly tense time, because the first generation of those born in a country that has been predominantly white before can then lay claim to that place as theirs, which begins to create a complex, messed-up idea of national identity. I've been reading Stuart Hall's description of immigrants as being like the Roman God Janus – one head looking back and the other looking forward, remaking the space in which they find themselves. That's what I was interested in, especially because I had recently been to Ghana, Jamaica and all those places which in many ways are my 'not-homes'. I was interested to be in a new context thinking about that.

I was very aware of my visibly 'other' body in these spaces and trying to think where it felt comfortable. Then, in Galway, I was in dialogue with a woman called Blessing who had come through the Irish immigration system, and its various violences, and had also been part of the live art installation *Exhibit B* by Brett Bailey when it was in Galway in 2015.

We spent a long time speaking about how that work might feel in Galway and how that might be different to how it felt in London or Edinburgh. I felt most of what I was doing was comparing these three positionalities. I don't know what comes next. It may turn into a piece of writing or a performance: something that speaks to solidarity rather than segmentation. But I don't know how to do that yet.

In that sense, place is always part of any collaborative project. My deep, dark fear would always be if I went to work in another context and just plonked myself down with no awareness of the struggles that are there. Especially being a British English artist when England has such a history of doing that. I think you have to be in dialogue and collaboration with the other artists there, and by being in collaboration with the artists you are already in dialogue with the place. Especially if you are transparent about your work being political.

At its best, collaborative work can reframe and re-contextualise a space. One of the other things Blessing and I were able to do was talk about what I, as a third or fourth generation black person in UK, have inherited from the activism of the generations before me. So, we are having an on-going conversation about how I might share that knowledge and experience with Blessing, and what a collaboration between me and young people in Galway might look like. Accepting we both come from different contexts but connecting those contexts. That's what I'm interested in. How can work be responsive rather than reactive.

Working with Blessing I was really aware I held the space for her, and this is what she valued and said felt essential and urgent. Maybe that's what art can do at its very best – hold space.

On international networks
As we have more of these complex international conversations, these collaborative spaces need to be rigorous and focused. The role of artists in something like CAPP is to recognise we are mirrors not only of our individual countries but of the continents we are a part of. We need to find ways to maintain conversations across borders, especially at a time when our governments are focused on making those borders more impenetrable. We need to think how we are going to do that in ways that are meaningful and don't make it feel like we as artists are in some strange crystal tower that separates us from our communities. What I have loved

about CAPP is having access to communities I wouldn't usually have had access to. If I had just gone out to Ireland with an artist commission, the dynamic would have been different – working collaboratively, bringing the international and the local together, enables politically urgent work to get done.

Mark Storor

On place

Art doesn't necessarily make place, but place can be – and in my case almost always is – a site for inspiration. Notions of place and 'place making' are often things that matter for organisations and institutions, but my work is never led by a desire to make place. Place already always exists. For me, it is always about the art. So much of the collaborative work we do transcends place. It articulates that which is felt but not always seen.

In some senses, I suppose art is less about making place than it is about revealing something – the place is there, what we do when we work together is reveal something that's greater than the limitations often imposed on a place. It's not enough, for me, to just record someone's story and document their lives. We need to open the space for stories to emerge, often through creating ritual.

On collaboration

Collaboration is something that has to be consistent and take place over a long period of time. Working collaboratively with people can often create a safe space to speak about things. Art often works 'between the lines', and, over time, can open up a portal into a space that didn't exist before, and that can be a making space. Whatever that making is, can allow us to look at things we can't always find a language for. Sometimes this means flying in the face of the 'official' narratives being told. When I'm working with someone, that space can become somewhere extraordinary, and things can happen as a result of that in many different ways.

My intention is never to be 'doing good' or making a place better, especially within structures that have proven to be harmful to people or don't work. I am interested in how we experience place, and create a space for the imagination and ideas and dreaming and inspiration and intuition to flourish. I'm interested in igniting or honouring or celebrating those things in us that are very present and alive and immediate. Creating experiences together that may inform, enhance or enrich our daily life.

On time

Commitment and time are crucial. We can't go in to a community or group of people and assume things: if we do we are in danger of peddling impoverished narratives that fit certain perceptions, sustained through seemingly intractable societal structures. But, if we spend time with people, the most precious and tender things can emerge. This doesn't mean they can't emerge quite quickly, but then you have to put in the time to earn the right to ask: "Can we work together on this?", and you can't ask that unless you've developed and earned trust.

On international networks

Connection with other cultures and other countries is vital. It can be the life blood of different ways of thinking, and encourage us to think in new and possibly revelatory ways. As far as making work is concerned, it can also add unusual, powerful colour, tone and texture to what we are doing. We can learn from one another and understand our humanity from different cultural perspectives through the work we make and share with each other.

Selina Thompson is an artist and performer based in Leeds. She undertook the three week Resort Residency at Lynders Mobile Home Park in North County Dublin villages and surrounding areas of Portrane and Donabate.

Franciso Rubio is a founding member of art collective LaFundició, a co-operative created in 2006 that promotes collective processes of knowledge construction, cultural practices and forms of relationship.

Mark Storor is an artist, working in the space between live art and theatre. His project, Baa Baa Baric Have You Any Pull?, is a 12 year undertaking in collaboration with the people of St Helens and Heart Of Glass.

Chrissie Tiller is a creative consultant and practitioner working across a range of sectors.

PARTNERS & PROJECTS

Agora Collective
Berlin, Germany

Workshops

Affect Module #1: Sensitive Observers
Stine Marie Jacobsen
Berlin, Germany

Affect Module #2: Exploring the Endotic
Lorenzo Sandoval
Berlin, Germany

Affect Module #3: Europe City in Berlin:
beyond the masterplan
Yves Mettler
Berlin, Germany

Affect Module #4: The artistic mission –
What is the role of an artist in a for-profit economy?
Diego Agulló
Berlin, Germany

Everything Under the Sun
Workshop #1: The Bakery
Egill Sæbjörnsson
Berlin, Germany

Everything Under the Sun Workshop #2:
Human Comma Being, The Dinner
Dafna Maimon
Berlin, Germany
Other partners involved
Nordic Culture Point,
Nordic Culture Fund

Affect Module #5: Mittelweg
Fotini Lazaridou-Hatzigoga
Berlin, Germany

Everything Under the Sun Workshop #6:
In Your Mind, Out of Your Body Experience
Hanne Lippard, Natasja Loutschko
Berlin, Germany

Everything Under the Sun Module #1:
Nordic Food Manifesto: From the
Backyard to the Table
Roderick Sloan, Kultivator
Berlin, Germany

Everything Under the Sun Module #2:
In the Age of FOODIE-ism
Tue Greenfort
Berlin, Germany

www.agoracollective.org
www.cappnetwork.com/author/agora

Residencies

Affect Module I: While We Work:
A Temporary State of Affairs
Judith Lavanga
Berlin, Germany

Affect Module II: The Artistic Mission: Dismantling
Professionalism in a For-Profit Economy?
Diego Agulló
Berlin, Germany

Affect Module III: The Institute for
Endotic Research: Reading Bodies
Lorenzo Sandoval
Berlin, Germany

Affect Module IV: Com(m)o(n) club radio:
time travel
Thelma Bonavita
Berlin, Germany

Affect Module V: On The Role of the Collective
in an Attention Economy
Sarah Margarita Lewis
Berlin, Germany

Affect Module VI: Conglomerate
Sol Calero, Ethan Hayes-Chute, Christopher
Kline, Derek Howard, Dafna Maimon
Berlin, Germany

Commissions

I am Hungry: Related Primates
Dafna Maimon
Berlin, Germany
Other partners involved
Nordic Culture Fund, KW Institut
for Contemporary Art and The Finnish
Institute in Germany

I am Hungry: [{"cibelle"(cavalli}bastos)]:
An embodied collective in (one) flux
Cibelle Cavalli Bastos
Berlin, Germany
Other partners involved
Cibelle Cavalli Bastos: Import Projects

"CAPP has been an incredible opportunity for a young, artist-run organisation such as ours. It has been extremely challenging to navigate through the institutionalisation of our project space, but the sense of generosity from the CAPP network definitely strengthened our beliefs and practices. I believe that the exchange generated within the four years has been an amazing learning process that deserves to continue in some shape or form."

Caique Tizzi
Artistic Director, Co-Founder

"Great experience! Especially through un-learning the usual 'listen-and-repeat' structure, and trying out how knowledge and critique can be embodied. I learned a lot."

Stine Marie Jacobsen
Affect 2015: Sensitive Observers

"It was a rare opportunity to work with a great team and try something I had been dreaming of for a long time: to assemble an ensemble of amateur performers, based on improvisation and exercises, involving food, dance, self-care and an array of absurd props and costumes."

Dafna Maimon
I am Hungry: Related Primates

"This workshop came at a convenient time; it felt like a great opportunity to meet like-minded people and deepen my practice."

Megan Wiessner
Affect 2015: Mittelweg facilitated by Fotini Lazaridou-Hatzigoga

"This process has helped me to find a way to develop my practice further; I feel that I can trust more in collaborative processes, because of the gentle and generous presence of this group."

Mariangela Tinelli
Affect 2015: Exploring the Endotic facilitated by Lorenzo Sandoval

www.agoracollective.org
www.cappnetwork.com/author/agora

Create
Dublin, Ireland

Workshops

The Machine of Death and Love
Gary Keegan (Brokentalkers)
The Gate Lab
Dublin, Ireland
Other partners involved
Dublin Dance Festival

DIY 12: Maps to Build Power
Adam James
The LAB and Dublin vicinity
Dublin, Ireland
Other partners involved
LADA and LAB Gallery
(Dublin City Council)

Strategies of Non Participation
Karen Mirza and Brad Butler
Fire Station Artists' Studios
Dublin, Ireland
Other partners involved
Fire Station Artists' Studios

Check Up, Check In
Jesse Jones and Eleanor Philips
The LAB
Dublin, Ireland
Other partners involved
artsandhealth.ie and the LAB Gallery
(Dublin City Council)

Youth Urban Design Workshops
Todo Por La Praxis
Callan, Co. Kilkenny, Ireland
Other partners involved
Callan Workhouse Union

Theatre of Our Bodies
Anna Furse
Dublin, Ireland
Other partners involved
Athletes of the Heart and Fringe Lab

www.create-ireland.ie
www.cappnetwork.com/author/create

Residencies

Resort Residency
Selina Thompson
Fingal, Ireland
Other partners involved
Fingal County Council Arts Office

Research Residency
Anna Furse
Dublin, Ireland
Other partners involved
Live Collision and Athletes of the Heart

*Artist In Residence at UCD College
of Social Science and Law 2017*
Sarah Browne
Dublin, Ireland
Other partners involved
UCD Parity Studios and UCD College
of Social Sciences and Law

Artist In Residence at UCD Parity Studios 2017
Glenn Loughran
Dublin, Ireland
Other partners involved
UCD Parity Studios and UCD College
of Social Sciences and Law

*Pathway 2 as part of The Lives We Live
public art programme*
Brokentalkers
Grangegorman, Dublin, Ireland
Other partners involved
Grangegorman Development Agency

Meet You at The Green?
Dan Dorocic
Callan, Co.Kilkenny, Ireland
Other partners involved
Callan Workhouse Union
and Trasna Productions

Research Residency
Sandra Noeth
Dublin and Limerick, Ireland
Other partners involved
Dublin Dance Festival and Dance Limerick

Commissions

Traveller Collection
Seamus Nolan
Dublin, Ireland
Other partners involved
Dublin City Gallery The Hugh Lane

I AM Not A Piece Of Meat
Anna Furse
Online as a digital artwork
Other partners involved
Athletes of the Heart

"CAPP offers an orientation towards the best kind of unknowing."

Seamus Nolan
Traveller Collection

"My involvement with CAPP through both residency and commission developed my work in medical communities, with Trinity College Anatomy Department and the Anatomy Department at Kings College, London. I collaborated with fantastic Dublin artists and technicians plus international collaborators. I'm extremely grateful to all at Create and Lynnette Moran (Lead Producer of CAPP to August 2017) for their support."

Anna Furse, *The Theatre of Our Bodies*,
Research Residency,
I AM Not A Piece Of Meat

"The sharing of arts practices is enjoyable and inspiring!"

Maud Hendricks
The Machine of Death and Love

"I have new thinking and ideas of political involvement and resistance, and how my practice in challenging (non-stable) environments might relate."

Marie Brett
Strategies of Non Participation

"CAPP has been such a significant project for Create. Working with our eight fantastic partners and all the artists has enriched our practice hugely as an organisation. Key principles of collaborative practice, such as negotiation, the importance of relationships and unlearning in order to learn more, have been to the fore in this project. And at its centre, the value and necessity of artistic practice and ideas in these times of change."

Ailbhe Murphy
Director

www.create-ireland.ie
www.cappnetwork.com/author/create

hablarenarte
Madrid, Spain

Workshops

If you don't pay attention to me,
I WILL NOT PAY ATTENTION TO YOU
Sarah Margarita Lewis
Huarte, Spain
Other partners involved
Centro Huarte, Centre for Contemporary
Art Production and AC/E

Do it twice
Fermín Jiménez Landa
San Sebastian, Spain
Other partners involved
Tabakalera, International Centre for
Contemporary Culture and AC/E

The Urban as Collective Space
Dos Jotas
Huarte, Spain
Other partners involved
Centro Huarte, Centre for Contemporary
Art Production and AC/E

Laboratory for Urban Recycling
Santiago Cirugeda
Vic, Spain
Other partners involved
ACVic, Centre for Contemporary Art
and AC/E

All together now
Zemos98 / hablarenarte
Madrid, Spain
Other partners involved
Medialab-Prado and AC/E

Ordinary Landscapes
Francesc Muñoz
Vic, Spain
Other partners involved
ACVic, Centre for Contemporary Art and AC/E

Collaborative Arts and Young People
Jennie Guy
San Sebastian, Spain
Other partners involved
Tabakalera, International Centre for
Contemporary Culture and AC/E

www.hablarenarte.com
www.cappnetwork.com/author/hablarenarte

Residencies & Commissions

Afluents
Seila Fernández Arconada and A+ Collective
Catalonya, Spain
Other partners involved
ACVic, Centre for Contemporary Art and AC/E

Rethinking the Container
Enter This Collective and Orekari Studio
Navarre, Spain
Other partners involved
Centro Huarte, Centre for Contemporary Art
Production and AC/E

Harrotu Ileak!
Felipe Polanía and Oihane Espuñez
San Sebastian, Spain
Other partners involved
Tabakalera, International Centre for
Contemporary Culture and AC/E

MANTA - Art, Fight and Learning
Alexander Ríos, Byron Maher and the
Union of Street Sellers and Can Collectors
Madrid, Spain
Other partners involved
Medialab-Prado and AC/E

"There's many undocumented people coming to Tabakalera. People come here to rest, and there is no need for the police to come here so often. I believe that with *Harrotu Ileak!*, Felipe and Oihane want to establish Tabakalera as a safe and open space. Some users don't seem to value that effort, but it would it would be a pity if this initiative does not work."

Anonymous, *Harrotu Ileak!*

"Exploring collective memory and emotional geographies is a good tool for recovering human relations and encouraging a greater social commitment to everyday surroundings. By activating those imagined spaces through the community itself, these tactics pave the way for more lasting work, and thus, a culmination of the re-placement process without need for architectural intervention."

Anna Recasens, *Afluents*

"Two totems are not the only result: they are part of the conclusions, a horizon of expectations, a tool that makes the debate or discussion something that can be told – one step in a long journey. More time is needed. This is just the beginning."

Javier García Clavel,
Rethinking the Container

"An intervention in a specific social setting is bound to generate idiomatic and cultural obstacles that are not easily overcome in a residency period. To avoid these, we fused residency and commission, and conceived them not so much as an occasion for developing a genuine artistic project, but instead as an opportunity for sharing methodologies with local agents from both artistic and social circles, which would take on those ideas in order to generate projects that would outlast CAPP."

Sören Meschede and Georg Zolchow
Producers

"Within *Harrotu Ileak!*, the challenge has been to create a space of trust where we can enter into a dialogue among equals. Our aim was to give the adolescent users of Tabakalera the chance to occupy the space not only passively, but also to engage them in generating their own proposals and activities."

Felipe Polanía, *Harrotu Ileak!*

"I think art has to generate a space of potentiality, to be non-prescriptive and activist. Socially engaged art presents us with an opportunity to avoid the choke-hold of neoliberal economic policies and to shed light on the unequal power structures society is bound by."

Warsame Ali Garare, *MANTA*

www.hablarenarte.com
www.cappnetwork.com/author/hablarenarte

Heart of Glass
St Helens, United Kingdom

Workshops

The Faculty
In Situ & Chrissie Tiller
St Helens, UK
Other partners involved
Super Slow Way, Creative Scene & LeftCoast

Prototype Projects: Artist Social
Led by Heart of Glass producer Emma Fry
St Helens, UK

Hunt and Darton: Are you Local?
Hunt and Darton
St Helens, UK
Other partners involved
Live Art Development Agency

Residencies

*With the Past in Front of me I walk Backwards
into the Future (Working Title / Project developed
into the Helen Programme)*
ANU Productions and Idle Women
Heart of Glass
St Helens, UK

Baa Baa Baric: Have You Any Pull?
A Quiet Revolution
Mark Storor
St Helens, UK
Other partners involved
St Peters C.E. Primary School, Rainford High
School, St Helens YMCA, Merseyside Police,
Change Grow Live St Helens and St Helens
Young Carers Association

20:20 Vision
Sophie Mahon
St Helens, UK
Other partners involved
Helena Homes, St Helens Youth Service, Wild
Card Amateur Boxing Club, St Cuthbert's
Catholic High School, St Augustine's of
Canterbury Catholic High School, The Sutton
Academy, Free Runners Derbyshire Hill Family
Centre, Parr Library, Chester Lane Library,
Holy Trinity Church and 818 group

www.heartofglass.org.uk
www.cappnetwork.com/author/heartofglass

Commissions

Bliss Park - Skate Park Project
Studio Morison
St Helens, UK
Other partners involved
St Helens Council, 51st Skate Shop and the
local skateboarding community

Baa Baa Baric: Have You Any Pull?
A Quiet Revolution
Mark Storor
St Helens, UK
Other partners involved
St Peters C.E. Primary School, Rainford High
School, St Helens YMCA, Merseyside Police,
Change Grow Live St Helens and St Helens
Young Carers Association

"Art is a way of making sense of the world, of exploring new possibilities and ways of being. The work of our communities, in collaboration with artists, has resulted in some remarkable projects being developed and delivered over the past number of years."

Patrick Fox
Director

"We are working as artists to re-establish aspects of civic life, helping local government and businesses fill the vacuum and claim back responsibility. We look to bring meaning, beauty and purpose into everyday life... Heart of Glass has given us the freedom to act as artists in order to reclaim these civic spaces for the whole community to use."

Heather Peak from Studio Morison
Bliss Park - Skate Park Project

"*Baa Baa Baric* was made up of 18 months of unique workshops, which led to a live art event. People are unpredictable. Remember: nothing you do is wrong; it's up to you how you engage with people. This is a one-off piece of magic."

Mark Storor
Baa Baa Baric: Have You Any Pull?
A Quiet Revolution

www.heartofglass.org.uk
www.cappnetwork.com/author/heartofglass

Kunsthalle Osnabrück
Osnabrück, Germany

Workshops

I DO - Gaining by Giving Up
Jakob & Manila Bartnik
Osnabrück, Germany

Werkstattschule (Workshop School)
Jorge Gonzalez
Osnabrück, Germany
Other partners involved
Ministry of Culture and Science
of Lower Saxony, Friedel and
Gisela Bohnenkamp Foundation

Residencies

You Are Splendid!
Maria Josè Arjona
Osnabrück, Germany
Other partners involved
Institute for Foreign Support (IFA),
Ministry for Science and Culture of Lower
Saxony, Friends of Kunsthalle Osnabrück

Systems of Weight
Ernesto Pujol
Osnabrück, Germany
Other partners involved
Ministry for Science and Culture of Lower
Saxony, Friends of Kunsthalle Osnabrück,
Landschaftsverband Osnabrücker Land e. V.

www.kunsthalle.osnabrueck.de
www.cappnetwork.com/author/kunsthalleosnabruck/

Commissions

The Rocket
David Rauer and
Joshua Sassmannshausen
Osnabrück, Germany

In & out
Roxy in the Box
Osnabrück, Germany

The Forgetting of Air
Francesca Grilli
Osnabrück, Germany

"This collaboration has shaped not only our programme, but also our mission. We have broadened our practices, including collaborative and participatory approaches. We reach out beyond the limits of the exhibition space into the neighbourhood, and into areas and communities with which we we have not been in contact previously."

Julia Draganovic
Director

"Great programme! It has been deeply enriching to exchange and discuss practical knowledge with other artists working in the collaborative field. It definitely improved and influenced our work. A benefit was also a new and wider public for participatory practice."

Jakob and Manila Bartnik
I DO - Gaining by Giving Up

"For me the fascination of this walking performance lay in the the challenge to find one's own rhythm, adapting it at the same time to that of the other participants."

Dagmar von Kathen
Part of Ernesto Pujol's
Systems of Weight performance

"We used many forms of communication to find everybody's artistic limits and then to exceed them. For me, one important aspect of these projects is that communication offers the chance for infinite learning, and participating in these projects gave me the chance to keep learning about my own and the collective body."

Francisca Marcus
Part of Ernesto Pujol's *Systems of Weight* performance and of *Forgetting of Air*, facilitated by Francesca Grilli

"The experience created the space to share ideas with the public about the exhibition, and exchange thoughts on migration, otherness, temporality and empathy. As a performance artist, I always look to understand what the viewer is experiencing, as this nourishes the possibility of creating strategies for interaction."

Maria Josè Arjona
You Are Splendid!

www.kunsthalle.osnabrueck.de
www.cappnetwork.com/author/kunsthalleosnabruck/

Live Art Development Agency
London, United Kingdom

Workshops

PLAYING UP
Sibylle Peters
London, UK
Other partners involved
Theatre of Research, Tate Early Years and
Families, Kids Best Biennial, Live Art UK,
Goethe Institut, Wapping High School

Between Menopause and Old Age
Rocio Boliver
London, UK
Other partners involved
Apiary Studios and Chelsea Theatre

DIY 12: Don't Wait Tables
Ursula Martinez
St Helens, UK
Other partners involved
Heart of Glass

DIY 12: SHADOW SECT
Shaun Caton
London, UK

DIY 12: Fans of Live Art
Owen G. Parry
London, UK
Other partners involved
Home Live Art, Whitechapel Studios

DIY 12: FAF - Female Armed Forces
Tania El Khoury & Abigail Conway
Norwich, UK
Other partners involved
Norwich Arts Centre

DIY 12: University of DIY
Katie Etheridge & Simon Persighetti
Manchester, UK
Other partners involved
Contact

DIY 12: Going Home
Geraldine Pilgrim
Cumbria, UK
Other partners involved
Abandon Normal Devices

DIY 12: Awkwoods
Daniel Oliver
London, UK

DIY 12: Maps To Build Power
Adam Jones
Dublin, Ireland
Other partners involved
Create

DIY 12: Eyes Wide Open -
Unearthing Fragments of the Future
Zierle & Carter with Christina Georgiou
Secret Location
Other partners involved
Live at LICA

www.thisisliveart.co.uk
www.cappnetwork.com/author/liveart/

Residencies

Restock, Rethink, Reflect 4:
Live Art, Privilege and the Young
Sibylle Peters
London, UK
Other partners involved
Theatre of Research

Restock, Rethink, Reflect 4:
Live Art, Privilege and the Old
Lois Weaver
London, UK
Other partners involved
InCompany

Restock, Rethink, Reflect 4:
Live Art, Privilege and the Displaced
Elena Marchevska
London, UK
Other partners involved
Counterpoints Arts

Restock, Rethink, Reflect 4:
Live Art, Privilege and Class
Kelly Green
London, Kent; UK
Other partners involved
Canterbury Christ Church University;
Sidney Cooper Gallery, Tate Exchange

Commissions

KAPUTT: Academy of Destruction
Sibylle Peters
London, UK
Other partners involved
Theatre of Research, Tate Early Years
and Families, Ark Academy

Untitled (Bodies)
Kira O'Reilly
London, UK; Dublin, Ireland; Helsinki, Finland

The Mansford Window
Sheaf+Barley
London, UK
Other partners involved
Simple Gifts

Declaration of Independence
Barby Asante
London and Liverpool
Other partners involved
Lois Weaver, Elena Marchevska,
Study Room In Exile

Scottee 10
Scottee
London and across the UK
Other partners involved
Roundhouse, Metal, Slung Low,
HOME, Camden People's Theatre,
Colchester Arts Centre

"CAPP was an opportunity for LADA to explore new partnerships, new territories and new ways of working. It was a testing ground for different forms of collaboration and it expanded our understanding of who collaborators can be. We have been able to reach new constituencies that will continue to inform our work for years to come."

Lois Keidan
Co-Director

"One of the most rewarding experiences I have ever had in my professional practice."

Owen G Parry
DIY 12: Fans of Live Art workshop

"It was a truly enriching experience to be able to work collaboratively with such talented artists, and to be inspired and informed by their vast and varied processes and modes of thinking and creating."

Shannon Mulvey
Tanja Ostojic's *Misplaced Women?* workshop, part of Elena Marchevska's *Live Art, Privilege and the Displaced* research residency

"Over the past few days, my favourite thing would have to be the people: how many people came in and how they left learning something about themselves and about destruction, which I think was very good. As an Academy, I think we have grown as people and changed our perspective."

Tolu (Principle Tolu the G.O.A.T.)
Academician at *KAPUTT: Academy of Destruction*

www.thisisliveart.co.uk
www.cappnetwork.com/author/liveart/

Ludwig Múzeum - Museum of Contemporary Art
Budapest, Hungary

Workshops

The Age of Participation
Anita Patonai, András Sereglei
Budapest, Hungary
Other partners involved
Káva Kulturális Műhely Egyesület
[Drama in Education Association]

Æctivators. Locally active architecture
Levente Polyák, Dénes Fajcsák
Budapest and Eger, Hungary
Other partners involved
KÉK Kortárs Építészeti Központ
[Contemporary Architecture Centre],
Arkt Építészeti Stúdió [Architecture Studio]

Residencies

Skubi and Bit.Fall
Miklós Tömör, Julius Popp
Budapest, Hungary
Other partners involved
Valyo Város és Folyó Egyesület [City and
Rives Association], DunaPest Festival

Commissions

Floating House
Bence Zsin
Pécs, Hungary
Other partners involved
Fogd a Kezem Alapítvány [Hold My Hand
Association], Pécsi Tudományegyetem
Művészeti Kar [University of Pécs Art Faculty]
and Pécs-Somogyi Iskola [Pécs–Somogyi
Primary School]

*"I Like Being a Farmer,
and I would like to stay one..."*
Antje Schiffers, Katalin Erdődi
Nagykamarás, Körösszegapáti, Szekszárd
Other partners involved
Sallai János, Kovács Orsolya,
Sárosdi Róbert, Sárosdi Judit

www.ludwigmuseum.hu/
www.cappnetwork.com/author/ludwigmuzeum/

Artists in Classrooms
Krisztina Erdei, Judit Fischer, Rokko Juhász,
Miklós Mécs, Miklós Soltis, Ágnes Szabics,
Zsófia Szemző, Dávid Utcai
Budapest, Hungary
Other partners involved
T-Tudok Tudásmenedzsment és Oktatáskutató
Központ Zrt. [T-Tudok Centre for Knowledge
Management and Educational Research
Inc.], GRUNDSULI Molnár Ferenc Magyar-
Angol Két Tanítási Nyelvű Általános Iskola
[Molnar Ferenc Hungarian-English Bilingual
Primary School], Hallássérültek Tanintézete
[Institution for People with Hearing
Difficulties]

Dragon Lee
András Tábori, Tamás Budha
Komló, Hungary
Other partners involved
Belső Tűz Egyesület [Inner Fire Association],
Komló Közösségek Háza [Community House
Komló], Gergely Tölgyfa, Zoltán Komlóczi

We Will See!
Emese Benczúr, Hajnalka Tarr,
Henrietta Szira, Kamilla Szíj,
Mariann Imre
Budapest, Hungary
Other partners involved
Vakok Állami Intézete
[Institute for Blind People]

To Be Continued?
Tibor Gyenis
Oszkó, Hungary
Other partners involved
Gyüttment Festival, Hegypásztor kör
[Vine Hill Sheperds' Circle], Sárkollektíva
[Mud Collective], Regio Earth Festival,
Hagyományos Házépítő Kft.
[Traditional House Building Ltd.]

Arboretum
Malvina Antal, Márk Kovács, Fanni Lakos,
Gergő Lukács, Viktória Makra,
Ádám Munkácsi, Kristóf Szabó
Budapest, Hungary
Other partners involved
Tamás Sándor Geröly, István Gőz, Ibolya
Juhász, Ágnes Németh, György László Pálfi,
Czakó Máté, Kőrösi Máté, Pro Progressione,
Műhely Alapítvány [Workshop Association]

"Creating an art piece via thinking with someone who has no connection to visual arts, forced me to leave my artistic comfort zone. This was a real challenge, well worth the experience artistically as well as on a personal development level."

Kamilla Szíj
We Will See!

"I feel that it was a great success that we could win the trust of local young people. Through our collaboration, however busy and challenging the period was, I see my own prejudices, possibilities and responsibilities in the system a lot clearer."

András Tábori, Gruppo Tökmag
Dragon Lee

"I was taking photos to document the events, but I could not resist getting involved more and more, so I became part of a large and important event. This feeling stayed with me after the exhibition opening as well."

Zoltán Selényi
Floating House

"We are thrilled with the success of our *Common Affairs* exhibition and the level of interest from all corners. New venues and creative solutions were born. Collaborative arts as a storage of creative questions and answers led us to the conclusion that Ludwig Múzeum can offer more space to these kind of practices."

Julia Fabényi, Director of Ludwig Múzeum - Museum of Contemporary Art

"I wanted to show people the whole picture, as often news about the troubles of watermelon farmers in the media is censored or distorted. I saw the project as an opportunity to talk about the reality of small producers and their struggles."

János Sallai, Watermelon producer from Nagykamarás, part of *I Like Being a Farmer and I Would Like to Stay One...*

www.ludwigmuseum.hu
www.cappnetwork.com/author/ludwigmuzeum

m-cult
Helsinki, Finland

Workshops

Kollab talkshops
Jussi Koitela, Arttu Merimaa,
Minna Tarkka
Helsinki, Finland

Dinner Games workshop
YKON (Christina Kral, Oliver
Kochta-Kalleinen, Pekko Koskinen)
Harakka Island, Finland
Other partners involved
Reception, the 1st triennial
of collaborative arts

Pleasures and Pains of Participation seminar
Oliver Kochta, Steve Maher,
Jouni Piekkari & al.
Helsinki, Finland
Other partners involved
ArtsEqual research initiative,
Reception - The 1st Triennial of Collaborative
Arts, Kiasma Contemporary Art Museum

Residences

Heavy Metal Detector
Steve Maher
Maunula, Finland
Other partners involved
Ten heavy metal bands
from the Helsinki region

Maunula Atmospheres
La Jetée (Paolo Patelli,
Giuditta Vendrame)
Maunula, Finland
Other partners involved
Maunula Media Workshop

Candy Stars
Juli Reinartz
Maunula, Finland
Other partners involved
Oulunkylä Congregation

I'm Talking to You
Elena Mazzi
Maunula, Finland
Other partners involved
Community Center Saunabaari

Our Coming Community
Valentina Karga
Maunula, Finland
Other partners involved
Saunabaari Ceramics group,
Maunula Upper Secondary School

Maunula (film)
Riikka Kuoppala & Thomas Martin
Maunula, Finland
Other partners involved
Maunula Media Workshop, Töyrytie Senior
Home, Maunula Primary School

www.m-cult.org
www.cappnetwork.com/author/mcult

Commissions

Sounds and Stories Live
Jobina Tinnemans
Maunula, Finland
Other partners involved
Saunabaari Community Center,
Maunula House

myfutures.trade
Eeefff: Dzina Zhuk, Nicolay Spesitsev
Maunula, Finland
Other partners involved
Maunula Youth House

Reform 75/100
Bernadette Wolbring
Maunula, Finland
Other partners involved
Saunabaari Community Center

Martial Law
Anastasia Artemeva
Maunula, Finland
Other partners involved
KRITS - Kriminaalihuollon tukisäätiö,
Helander home

Recovered Utopias
Axel Straschnoy
Maunula, Finland
Other partners involved
Maunula Upper Secondary School,
Aalto University Media Factory

Partizaning Maunula
Partizaning (Anton Polskiy,
Natalia Sinitsina)
Maunula, Finland
Other partners involved
Aalto University / VICCA programme,
Maunulan Sanomat newspaper

Maunula Looks
Rogério Nuno Costa & Jaime Culebro
Maunula, Finland
Other partners involved
Maunula House

Avatar Influence Game
Tellervo & Oliver Kalleinen
Maunula, Finland
Other partners involved
Maunula House

Memory Switch
Johanna Raekallio & Babak Arzani
Maunula, Finland
Other partners involved
Metsälä Refugee Centre, Maunula House

Maunula's New Clothes
Otto Karvonen & Justus Kantakoski
Maunula, Finland
Other partners involved
Saunabaari Community Center,
Helsinki City Adult Education Centre

"In Maunula, we are starting broader research through an experimental project. We are looking at environments as media, because they hold a latent image of our society, our civilisation. We will look at the skies, because we see them as a commons, a background shared by the whole community, by each individual– and that belongs to everyone."

La Jetée
(Paolo Patelli & Giuditta Vendrame)
Maunula Atmospheres

"We are originally from India and our daughter didn't have enough chance to mingle with the local people. This gave her an opportunity to speak not just with kids but with different age groups. Also it helped to develop thinking ability about what the future should look like, and how to work in a group in a multicultural environment."

Rahul Chalrewar (father of participant)
Maunula (film)

"I hope that our coming community would be one of equality, and on the other hand, because equality kind of comes from the outside, the we should be peers, so that 'peer equality' would be our common value."

Eila Hämäläinen
(speaking on project video)
Our Coming Community

www.m-cult.org
www.cappnetwork.com/author/mcult

Tate Liverpool
Liverpool, United Kingdom

Workshops

The Reflective Practitioner
Chrissie Tiller
St Helens and Liverpool, UK
Other partners involved
Heart of Glass

SEE, THINK, DO
Quad Collective
Liverpool, UK
Other partners involved
Liverpool John Moores University,
Useful Art Association, Heart of Glass

Visible Art Award
Visible/Tate Liverpool
Liverpool, UK
Other partners involved
Visible Research programme,
Liverpool City Council

The Cartography Project
Britt Jurgensen, Samatha Jones Homebaked;
Nina Edge(Welsh Streets and Granby Four
Streets); Christopher Kline; Amy Worsley;
Charlotte Richardson; Raphaella Davies
Liverpool, UK
Other partners involved
Digital Learning, Tate Modern

Collaborative Conversations
Britt Jurgensen, Homebaked; Shaun Curtis,
METAL Culture; Vic McEwan, The Harmonic
Oscillator; Liz Wewiora, Open Eye Gallery;
Emily Gee, FACT; Nina Edge (Welsh Streets
and Granby Four Streets)
Liverpool, UK
Other partners involved
Liverpool John Moores University

www.tate.org.uk/liverpool
www.cappnetwork.com/author/tateliverpool

Residences

Art Gym
Tate Collective, Assemble
Liverpool, UK

Commissions

O.K. - The Musical
Christopher Kline
Liverpool, UK
Other partners involved
Super Slow Way, Pennine Lancashire
Burnley, Lancashire

"*O.K. - The Musical* was a highlight of the CAPP programme for Tate Liverpool, encapsulating a collaborative practice that was based on trust, openness and generosity from the artist and all those who took part. Everyone responded to an invitation that was sincere, and brought their own stories, knowledge and skills to create a 'temporary' theatre and community. It was a joyous and moving experience and one that has generated new relationships that are now ongoing."

Lindsey Fryer
Head of Learning/Curator

"This project challenged everyone to work together but there was a great sense of collective achievement in the final performances. Many children, young people and adults have been inspired to continue to pursue their interests in creative activity. It provided a communal creative space where people from all backgrounds could feel comfortable contributing ideas and skills."

Raphaella Davies
O.K. - The Musical

"*O.K.* has been a transcendent experience for me, and it's been an absolute privilege to work with the many people of Liverpool and Burnley who collaborated on this project in a myriad of ways. From the choir to the quilters to the Tate staff, we all came together as a community with surprising urgency."

Christopher Kline, *O.K. - The Musical*

"The challenge of learning so many songs so quickly and performing them as part of a larger show really saw our members step up. We were capable of achieving more than we'd ever challenged ourselves to do before. Together, we grew in confidence and skill, and it's given us the self-belief to keep challenging ourselves ever since. The experience has been a huge milestone in our development."

Ema Quinn, Choir with No Name
O.K. - The Musical

"*O.K. - The Musical* at Tate Liverpool was a fantastic opportunity for students from The City of Liverpool College to participate in an external collaborative artwork in an amazing professional environment. This experience not only developed their artistic techniques, their organisational skills and confidence , but also gave them a real understanding of the power of collective expression."

Tracey Brown, City of Liverpool College
O.K. - The Musical

www.tate.org.uk/liverpool
www.cappnetwork.com/author/tateliverpool

Acknowledgements

As project lead and Director I would first like to extend my deep appreciation and thanks to the team at Create who have delivered CAPP with such commitment and enthusiasm. I would also like to thank those who have left the organisation for their contributions to the CAPP project: Patrick Fox who initiated this journey, and Lynnette Moran and Katrina Goldstone for their respective work up to August 2017.

On behalf of Create I would also like to thank our national partners who were essential to realising the programme in Ireland, and gratefully acknowledge our funders: the Arts Council of Ireland, the Department of Culture, Heritage and the Gaeltacht, and Dublin City Council. As lead partner, Create warmly thanks our colleagues in the eight partner organisations with whom we have had the good fortune to work with so closely over the past four years.

On behalf of the CAPP network, for their contribution to this publication, sincere thanks to Megan Vaughan, editor Eleanor Turney and designer David Caines. To our three essay contributors, Dr. Mick Wilson, Prof. Eleonora Belfiore and Dr. Aida Sánchez de Serdio Martín for their insightful analysis and critical contributions. To artist and researcher Dr. Susanne Bosch for her essay and contribution to CAPP since its inception. We also wish to thank the partner conveners and artists who took the time to engage in the dialogue series.

Finally our sincere thanks to those community members, activists, residents, thinkers, participants and co-authors who shaped the programme through their collaborations with CAPP artists. And lastly, a great debt is owed to all those artists who worked with us to devise and facilitate professional development workshops, engage in residencies, deliver commissions and enrich our thinking at various partner meetings and Staging Posts, making CAPP the incredible journey that it has been.

Ailbhe Murphy, Director, Create. May 2018.

COLLABORATIVE
ARTS PARTNERSHIP
PROGRAMME

The Collaborative Arts Partnership Programme (CAPP) is a transnational cultural programme (2015 - 2018) focusing on the field of collaborative and socially engaged arts practice across art-form and context. CAPP comprises a nine-organisation network, led by Create, the national development agency for collaborative arts in Ireland.

CAPP is a diverse range of dynamic cultural and artistic organisations supporting the development of artistic projects of excellence. Partners include: Agora Collective (Germany), Create lead partner (Ireland), hablarenarte (Spain), Heart of Glass St Helens (UK), Kunsthalle Osnabrück (Germany), Live Art Development Agency (UK), Ludwig Museum, Museum of Contemporary Art (Hungary), m-cult (Finland), and Tate Liverpool (UK).

The overall goal of CAPP is to improve and open up opportunities for artists who are working collaboratively across Europe, by enhancing mobility and exchange whilst at the same time engaging new publics and audiences for collaborative practices. The different strands of the CAPP programme consist of national and international professional development opportunities, artist residencies, commissioned works, touring and dissemination, and a major showcase in Dublin (Ireland) 2018.

cappnetwork.com

Co-funded by the
Creative Europe Programme
of the European Union

The European Commission support for the production of this publication does not constitute an endorsement of the contents which reflects the views only of the authors, and the Commission cannot be held responsible for any use which may be made of the information contained therein.

With the support of

COLLABORATIVE
ARTS PARTNERSHIP
PROGRAMME

www.cappnetwork.com

The CAPP website includes fuller information about all the artists
and projects discussed in this volume, plus a collection of digital
resources aimed at practitioners, scholars and institutions working
in communities or with an otherwise socially engaged ethos.

The texts from this publication can also be accessed in translation,
in Finnish, German, Hungarian and Spanish.